Advance praise for *A Teen's Guide to Going Vegetarian*

▼▼▼▼▼▼▼▼▼▼▼▼▼

A sound guide for teens in the dietary jungle of America."
—Walter C. Willett, M.D., Chair,
Department of Nutrition, Harvard School of Public Health

If you want to be hardcore about anything, this is it: Watch what you put in your mouth. This book is comprehensive and not boring."
—Michael Stipe, R.E.M.

Judy Krizmanic speaks to the evolving teenager like a knowledgeable, caring friend— providing key insights at a crucial juncture in the young person's life. I wish I had this book when *I* was fourteen and pondering the very same issues. I will recommend this book to my lecture audiences."
—Michael Klaper, M.D.,
author of *Vegan Nutrition: Pure and Simple*

Teens and their families will enjoy the fun-loving and energetic style of this book. Packed with sound, sensible nutrition information, *A Teen's Guide to Going Vegetarian* will help them feel confident about making the switch to a more healthful, environmentally friendly lifestyle."
—Suzanne Havala, M.S., R.D., author of *Simple, Lowfat & Vegetarian*

Breaking away from meat and dairy products can give today's kids the power to avoid tomorrow's health problems. *A Teen's Guide to Going Vegetarian* makes the transition easy and fun. It identifies the obstacles young people face in changing their diets and shows how to deal with them. Nutritional issues are covered in detail, which will reassure parents as well."
—Neal D. Barnard, M.D., President,
Physicians Committee for Responsible Medicine, and author of *Food for Life*

Teens concerned about their own health, or the well-being of animals and the environment, should consider going vegetarian. This book is a great guide to get you started."
—Michael F. Jacobson, Ph.D., Executive Director,
Center for Science in the Public Interest

A very useful guide."
—Dean Ornish, M.D., Director,
Preventive Medicine Research Institute, and author of *Eat More, Weigh Less*

I gave the manuscript to my twelve-year-old neighbor, who has recently gone vegetarian. She found the nutrition part very useful, liked the recipes she tried, and thought it altogether very helpful for someone who is considering being vegetarian, a wonderful book to read.' can think of no higher recommendation."
—Annemarie Colbin, C.H.E.S.,
founder of the Natural Gourmet Cookery School, New York City,
and author of *Food and Healing*

A TEEN'S GUIDE TO GOING VEGETARIAN

by **Judy Krizmanic**

Illustrations by Matthew Wawiorka

Foreword by T. Colin Campbell, Ph.D.,
Jacob Gould Schurman Professor of
Nutritional Biochemistry, Cornell University

PUFFIN BOOKS

Dedicated to my family, especially to
Lorraine Krizmanic—my mother and my friend

PUFFIN BOOKS
Published by the Penguin Group
Penguin Books USA Inc., 375 Hudson Street, New York, New York 10014, U.S.A.
Penguin Books Ltd, 27 Wrights Lane, London W8 5TZ, England
Penguin Books Australia Ltd, Ringwood, Victoria, Australia
Penguin Books Canada Ltd, 10 Alcorn Avenue, Toronto, Ontario, Canada M4V 3B2
Penguin Books (N.Z.) Ltd, 182–190 Wairau Road, Auckland 10, New Zealand

Penguin Books Ltd, Registered Offices: Harmondsworth, Middlesex, England

First published in the United States of America by Viking,
a division of Penguin Books USA Inc., 1994
Simultaneously published in Puffin Books

1   3   5   7   9   10   8   6   4   2

PUBLISHER'S NOTE
The ideas and information contained in this book are not intended
as a substitute for consulting with a physician. All matters regarding
health require medical supervision.

The Library of Congress has cataloged the Viking edition as follows:
Krizmanic, Judy.
A teen's guide to going vegetarian / by Judy Krizmanic ; illustrations by Matthew
Wawiorka ; foreword by T. Colin Campbell.   p.   cm.
Includes bibliographical references and index.
ISBN 0-670-85114-0 (alk. paper)
1. Vegetarianism—Juvenile literature.   2. Vegetarian cookery—Juvenile literature.
3. Youth—Nutrition—Juvenile literature.
[1. Vegetarianism.   2. Vegetarian cookery.   3. Nutrition.]
I. Wawiorka, Matthew, ill.   II. Title.
TX392.K75   1994   613.2'62—dc20   94-7790   CIP   AC

Puffin Books ISBN 0-14-036589-3

Printed in the United States of America
Set in Utopia

CONTENTS

ACKNOWLEDGMENTS

This book contains anecdotes, information, and inspirations from many sources. Thanks to everyone who contributed in some way. Deserving of particular thanks are the countless young people who so willingly shared their personal stories with me; each one helped shape the information on the following pages. Thanks to all of you for being so adventuresome and for enduring my seemingly endless questions about your eating habits—a rather bizarre topic to talk about with someone you've never met before. Special thanks to Fernando, Rachel, Lynnise, and Heather in Chicago, and to Tauna Houghton, her family, and the whole Meatless in Seattle crew. Special thanks to Sonnet Pierce, an aspiring young chef from rural Missouri, for supplying the original recipes that appear in chapter 13.

The task of finding these young vegetarians was a real grassroots effort. Thanks to all the vegetarian societies who helped me seek out my sources, as well as anyone who may have passed along the name of that vegetarian niece, babysitter, or friend of a friend of a friend.

As I worked on this book, I was reminded again of the generosity and compassion of the folks who spend their lives teaching others about vegetarian issues. Many people and groups have happily shared their resources and put me in touch with the proper sources. Greatest thanks to Sally Clinton of the Vegetarian Education Network—the ultimate voice on vegetarian teendom. Thanks to Debra Wasserman and Charles Stahler of the Vegetarian Resource Group, Brian Graff of the North American Vegetarian Society, and all of my wonderful friends at *Vegetarian Times* magazine (especially Terry for helping me to track down articles, and Karin for suggesting some of the historical quotes). Thanks also to Clare Obis for the input on feminism.

On the environmental front, thanks to Alan Durning of Worldwatch Institute for sharing his work and for reviewing mine, to John Robbins and everyone at the EarthSave Foundation, and to Lynn Jacobs of the Ranching Task Force. Thanks to Zoe Weil of Animalearn, Gene Bauston (and Lorri, and all at the Farm Sanctuary), and Jim Mason for reviewing the chapter on animals and factory farms, and to everyone at People for the Ethical Treatment of Animals for their constant readiness with resources and info. Thanks to Jay Dinshah of the American Vegan Society and Lewis G. Regenstein for providing information about vegetarians and the religions of the world. Thanks to Susan Campbell at EarthSave for reviewing the chapter on school issues, and to others who in some way contributed to this section: Todd Winant, Dorothy Pannell, Susan Davis-Allen, Gail Heebner, and Pat Graham. Thanks too to vegetarian educator Jon Schottland, who agreed to meet with me in Brattleboro on one of Vermont's coldest winter days.

On matters of vegetarian health and nutrition, I have had the pleasure of receiving input and advice from some of the best in the field. Thanks to all who reviewed the chapters on health and nutrition: To Virginia Messina, M.P.H., R.D., who also provided the daily food guide and menu framework found in chapter 10, Mark Messina, Ph.D., Michael Klaper, M.D., and Suzanne Havala, M.S., R.D. Also thanks to Patricia Johnston, Ph.D., R.D., Susan Lark, M.D., Reed Mangels, Ph.D., R.D., Graydon Yatabe, and Bill Hottinger. Special thanks to

T. Colin Campbell, Ph.D., for writing the foreword and for inspiring me immensely through his own work.

It has been more than two years since Lisa Pliscou first contacted me from Viking to invite me to write a book for vegetarian teens. Lisa's inspired vision, unwavering enthusiasm, and insightful editing are what really brought this project to life. Thanks to Lisa for making it so much fun, and to all at Viking for knowing that it was time for this book.

There are many people whose influences may not be as tangible to the reader but who have been most significant to me. Thanks and love to my family: To my mother, Lorraine, for unwavering love, support, patience, and willingness to try new things (like leaving the eggs out of the cookies and eating fake turkey with me on Thanksgiving). Warm thanks to my sister, Anna, and to Matt, Kate, and Kyle; to my brother, John, and to Alicia, Bobby, and Gabriele—it's great being the nutty vegetarian in all of your lives. Thanks also to Sharon, Chuck, Beth, and Mark Weingarten for all of the encouragement.

This book was also written with the memory of my father, Robert, in my heart.

I'm lucky to have more supportive friends than I can mention, but you know who you are. Regards to all who listened to sentences and commented on my cadence (Suz), and who pitched me wacky, wonderful title ideas (sorry no *9021Okra*, Roger). Thanks to Anna Balla for the beautiful veggie drawings upon my walls. Particular thanks and much peace to Paul Obis for introducing me to the vegetarian world; I can see out my window the exact site on the beach where you started up *Vegetarian Times* twenty years ago. Thanks to Mark and to

Sally, for teaching me much. And to Debra: Lucky, lucky me for knowing you.

And of course: Big, big thanks to Bill Weingarten and Aiko, companions by my side. It's a charmed life. Bill, thank you for encouraging me to be me and to write what I write, for keeping me going, and for sampling all that snackin' cake. (*And* for reading through the manuscript with me, word for word, when I had lost all sense of how it sounded.) I love sharing our lives and our work. Your editing, your advice, and your simply being around made this a much better book. Aiko, as always, you're such a goo'boy.

FOREWORD

When I was invited to write this foreword, I had to stop and reflect. It was not because of a fear of supporting an idea without scientific basis; instead I was struck by the realization that the idea behind this book—that going vegetarian can be one of the most healthful choices a teenager can make—had come so far so fast in so few years.

In the early seventies, scientists and national policymakers (and much of the general public) regarded vegetarianism as something rather esoteric or even kooky. Then, during the late seventies and early eighties, attitudes began to shift. Senator George McGovern's Select Committee on Nutrition held a series of hearings on diet and heart disease and concluded that the average American diet was too high in red meat and fat (on the average about 38–40 percent of total calories), and too low in vegetables, fruit, and complex carbohydrates. The prestigious National Academy of Sciences invited a group of scientific experts to review the evidence on diet and cancer; the academy reached the same conclusion. And when the U.S. Surgeon General warned the public of the link between cigarette smoking and lung cancer, he added that diets containing more foods of plant origin made good nutritional sense.

Each of these investigations was based on reviews of thousands of scientific studies. The very fact that they took place indicated that scientists and policymakers had begun to take increasing notice of the evidence concerning the nutritional value of eating foods from the plant kingdom—and of its implications to public health.

These reports, however, although moving in the right direction, are now believed not to have gone far enough in their recommendations that Americans decrease their dietary fat to about 30 percent of total calories. That's not much of a change, especially if all one does is to continue to eat animal foods—just lower-fat versions—rather than increase the quantity of low-fat plant foods. Close examination of these reports reveals a significant, if tacit acknowledgment: that the scientific evidence suggests that the healthiest diets would be much more vegetarian in nature (and much lower in total fat).

And now, in the nineties, it is generally known that such diets are capable not only of helping to prevent certain diseases that kill millions of Americans prematurely, but also of improving health even in early life. A vegetarian diet has been shown to prevent the accumulation of plaque (the stuff that eventually gives rise to cardiovascular disease) in blood vessels, even in young children. A vegetarian diet can go hand in hand with physical fitness and promote a healthy appearance. It can set a young person on the road to good dietary practices for the rest of life.

Unfortunately, the food that is available to our country's children does not always reflect the scientific evidence described above, although a growing number of people are pushing for more healthful fare in settings such as the school cafeteria. It is encouraging to see young people making their *own* healthful changes and empowering themselves by becoming vegetarians. Ironically, while some parents worry that a vegetarian diet is (at best) just another fad, or (even worse) unhealthy, it is actually one of the most responsible and nutritionally sound things a teenager can do.

Judy Krizmanic lists some very famous people who are intellectual, artistic, and athletic role models—and also vegetarians. Nowadays, many athletes who aspire to championship-level competition know that a vegetarian diet can help sustain their physical fitness. Incidentally, the term "vegetarian" is based on the Latin root *vegetus*, which does not mean vegetable, as so many people think, but vigorous. Truly food for thought.

It is my belief that this book amply serves young people who are interested in becoming vegetarians. I hope that it will also inspire them to strive for good health—for themselves, for their society, and for their planet.

—T. Colin Campbell, Ph.D.,
Jacob Gould Schurman Professor of Nutritional Biochemistry,
Cornell University

A TEEN'S GUIDE TO GOING VEGETARIAN

INTRODUCTION

~~~~~~~~~~~~~Quick. Name a few vegetarians.

Here are some names to get you thinking: Hank Aaron, Thomas Edison, Mahatma Gandhi, Eddie Vedder, k. d. lang, Jerry Garcia, Mr. Rogers, Christie Brinkley, Henry David Thoreau. (What a mix!)

Can't come up with any more names? Hint: Don't think celebrity. Think people you know. Chances are, some of your friends and classmates are going vegetarian. Or at least thinking about it.

Teens everywhere are becoming vegetarians. *Everywhere.* In New York City and in rural Missouri. In El Paso, Texas, and in Seattle, Washington. In Honolulu, Hawaii, and in Monroe, Michigan. All over Canada, too.

Here's a typical story: Last Fourth of July in Chicago, 16-year-old vegetarian Andrea Arnold attended the Lollapalooza III concert fest with thousands of other people. And was *she* surprised. "I was shocked by the vast number of teens who have joined me in ridding animals from their diet." Andrea figured she'd have to search high and low at the festival for something, *anything,* without meat. But it wasn't just burgers and hot dogs for *this* concert crowd. Amid the music and dancing, Andrea found stands selling vegetable-filled turnovers, meatless spaghetti, and eggplant sandwiches. "This was a mainly 'teenage' event, but many of the booths were vegetarian. That must mean there are many of us!"

She's right. There are. All across America, young people are saying that it's time for a change. Time to reset the table. Time to replace cheeseburgers with veggie burgers, sausage pizza with spinach pizza, chicken Parmesan with tofu potpie.

Vegetarianism is hot, hot, hot. You can tell just by looking around (ever notice how many more meatless dishes you'll find on a menu lately?). Or you can look at the statistics: More than 12 million Americans call themselves vegetarians, says *Vegetarian Times* magazine. It's not clear *exactly* how many of today's vegetarians are teens, but trend-trackers say that your generation is probably the fastest-growing segment of the veggie population. And there are plenty of signs that the number is already huge: There's a national newsletter, for instance, just for vegetarian teens (written *by* vegetarian teens). Big-name publications like *The New York Times, The Boston Globe, The Washington Post,* and *U.S. News & World Report* have printed stories about this spreading phenomenon of meatless minors. You'll even see shows about veggie teens on MTV.

And, as Andrea found, you'll bump into vegetarians your age wherever you turn.

Thirteen-year-old Joseph Weisenthal, who has been a vegetarian all his life, says he's seen the ranks of vegetarians growing. "A few years ago, I wouldn't have come across very many. But now if I tell someone I'm a vegetarian, they might know of other people who are vegetarians, too."

With so many vegetarians around, people are getting more comfortable with the concept. In fact, people won't look at you so strangely anymore when they find out you're a vegetarian. Instead, they'll probably say something like, "Oh, I don't eat much meat anymore myself." People know it's a healthy choice. And who doesn't want to be hip? As Julie, a 19-year-old vegetarian, has noticed, "It's almost like people admire you for it."

This book is all about why so many people your age are going vegetarian and how you can, too. We'll start with the *why*. Some people do it because it's a cool thing to do. But, as it turns out, most teens become vegetarians for really meaningful, well thought-out—and sometimes pretty intense—reasons. You'll meet people like Fernando and Rachel, whose workshop teaches why a vegetarian diet can be better for the planet. You'll meet Erin and David, who say that they have really strong feelings about the way cows, chickens, and pigs are raised. You'll meet Cara and Gautam, who have deep ethical concerns about eating animals. The way they see it, food is more than something you eat when you're hungry: What you eat affects the world around you.

These teens love being vegetarians because it gives them a chance to take a stand, speak out, make a difference. Of course, they all know that you can't fix everything that's wrong in the world just by changing the way you eat. There are big problems—crime, violence, prejudice, hatred—that are not going to go away just because you choose a veggie burger over a Big Mac. But they say that if the reasons for being a vegetarian make sense to you, it's a place you may want to start fixing what you *can.*

Most of this book is about lighter stuff. There are plenty of people who say that being a vegetarian is just plain fun. Bonus: It's something that's really good for you, too.

We'll get down to the nuts and bolts of how *you* can be a vegetarian. Sure, there are other books about vegetarianism, but it can be hard to find answers to *your* questions, like: What if my parents freak out when I tell them I'm going to be a vegetarian? Why doesn't my school serve veggie burgers instead of that gross meatloaf? What do I do when my friends' parents invite me over to dinner? What kinds of meals can I make quickly after school? These are the kinds of things we'll cover. And other things, too: It's quite possible that you've never had to shop or cook for yourself in the past, but as a vegetarian you might have to. "And I've never quite figured out what nutrients I need and where I'm supposed to get them," says one vegetarian. In the following pages, you'll learn what foods are good for you, where to find them, and how to make them into meals. A lot of people have the misconception that a teen couldn't possibly be aware enough or responsible enough to know about such things. Here are some tools to help you prove them wrong.

So, let's roll up our sleeves and get ready for action. There are many good reasons to go vegetarian, and it's easy to do.

But remember that although this book offers suggestions and advice—and that many teens *are* going vegetarian—it's your choice. "If you're thinking of being a vegetarian, just try it," says Michelle, an 18-year-old vegan. "Test the water. See how you feel. Vegetarianism might not be for everyone. But it's worth it to see how it feels to you."

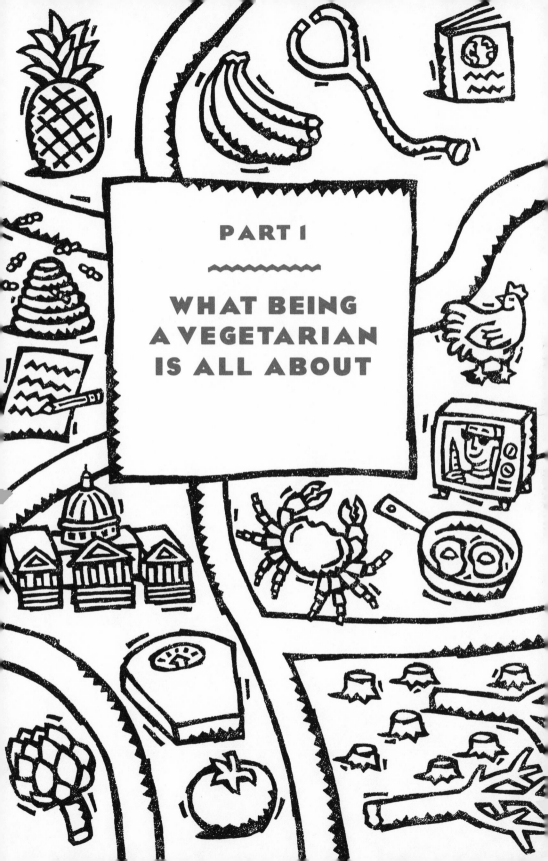

PART I

WHAT BEING A VEGETARIAN IS ALL ABOUT

CHAPTER 1

WHAT IS A VEGETARIAN, ANYWAY?

" I am a great eater of beef, and I believe that does harm to my wit. "
—**William Shakespeare**, Twelfth Night *(I, iii)*

First things first. What, exactly, is a vegetarian?

Hmm. Maybe you have a friend who says she's a vegetarian. You've noticed that she doesn't eat the burgers or fried chicken in the school cafeteria, but once you saw her eat a fish sandwich. One "vegetarian" you know eats chicken sometimes. Another vegetarian you know of doesn't eat any beef, chicken, or fish at all. And you know that some vegetarians don't even eat eggs or cheese. Who's the real vegetarian?

Well, the nice thing about being a vegetarian is that you can go about it in many, many ways. But we should start with a basic definition, so we know what we're talking about here. *A vegetarian is someone who eats no meat of any kind*—no beef, no pork, no poultry, no fish. As mentioned above, the term *vegetarian* is sometimes used pretty loosely by people who have all different types of diets.

Actually, there are specific names to describe the various sorts of vegetarians. This is a good time to run through them:

VARIOUS VARIETIES OF VEGETARIANS

VEGETARIAN: *This is the most commonly used term, and it means a diet that doesn't contain any meat (beef, pork, poultry, seafood). It may include other animal products such as eggs, milk, cheese, and honey.*

OVO-LACTO VEGETARIAN: *This is sort of scientific-sounding, but it's actually just a more accurate name for the type of diet described above.* Ovo *means that this is a vegetarian diet that includes eggs;* lacto *means the diet includes milk products.*

LACTO-VEGETARIAN: *A vegetarian diet that includes milk products but no eggs. This type of diet is popular in India, where many people are vegetarians for spiritual reasons.*

OVO-VEGETARIAN: *You guessed it: This diet includes eggs but no milk products. (This type of diet isn't all that common.)*

VEGAN *(pronounced VEE-gun)*: *Most people use the word* vegan *to describe a diet that omits all animal products, including meat, eggs, dairy products, and honey (although some people who call themselves vegans do eat honey). Some vegans you meet will wear leather and other animal products, but many vegans won't. Note: The American Vegan Society says that the term vegan should be reserved for a person who does not use animal products for food or clothing (no leather, wool, silk, or goose down); according to the AVS, the word* vegan *describes not just a diet but a whole lifestyle that avoids all forms of animal exploitation.*

SEMI-VEGETARIAN: *This term is sort of vague, because it could mean a number of things. It might mean someone who eats meat sometimes, like on Thanksgiving. It might also describe someone who doesn't eat one kind of meat—say, beef—but does eat another kind—say, chicken or fish. You might hear people use more specific terms such as pesco-vegetarian (eats fish) or pollo-vegetarian (eats chicken). A lot of vegetarians say these terms don't make much sense, since fish and chicken are animals, and animal flesh is meat. The way they see it, you're either a vegetarian or you're not.*

STRICT VEGETARIAN: *This is another sort-of-confusing term that doesn't have just one meaning. It's sometimes used to describe a person who doesn't eat any animal products at all (like a vegan), but it* *might also be used to describe any kind of vegetarian who has a strong commitment to a particular diet (in other words, a person who still eats dairy products might be "strict" about not eating meat).*

MACROBIOTIC: *This is a diet philosophy of Japanese origin. It is mostly vegetarian but may include fish. A macrobiotic diet is based on specific principles rather than specific foods. For instance, its guidelines say that you should eat foods that are native to the region where you live, and that you should balance certain types of foods with others.*

NATURAL HYGIENE: *This sounds more like a brand of soap than a way of eating, but if you read a lot about healthy eating, you might have heard of this. Actually, it describes a whole lifestyle, not just a type of diet. The idea is to promote the best health possible, through things like fresh air, sunshine, rest, good relationships, and a diet centered around fruits, vegetables, beans, nuts, and seeds. Raw foods are considered especially good.*

FRUITARIAN: *You might have heard of this really extreme way of eating. But note: Health experts warn that it's not an appropriate diet. Fruitarians eat—you guessed it—fruit, which, by definition, actually includes things such as squash, seeds, and nuts as well as things like oranges and apples.*

All of these definitions can sound pretty confusing. Ovo-this, lacto-that. After reading through these terms, you might be left wondering exactly where you fit in. Try not to worry too

much about what label suits you. These words are just that—
labels. It is important to have some standard definitions to
follow, but the main purpose of these definitions is simply to
help you communicate with other people about your diet.
And anyway, what's more important than the label is what
motivates you to wear it in the first place.

WHY BE A VEGETARIAN?

So much for what a vegetarian diet is. But why on earth would
someone become one? Actually, there are lots of reasons.
Here's a quick overview.

Some people are vegetarian because they believe it's better
for the environment. "I'm aware of the effect it would have if
everyone cut back on meat consumption," says 16-year-old
Jeremy Blackman of Seattle. "When people start eating so
much meat that it's having such an effect on the environment,
it's like, Enough! Time to reconsider!" Although skipping a
burger here and there isn't going to solve all the planet's problems, it's a start. "It's a very powerful statement," says Jade
Thome, 19. "Being able to change yourself—and stick to it—is
a statement that you are able to make a commitment to a better environment."

Some people are vegetarian for the animals. "I completely
disagree with the cruel way that animals are raised and
slaughtered," says Samantha Updegrave, 16, of Pennsylvania.
As she sees it, it's not necessary to kill animals just so people
can eat them. Concern for the animals appears to be the
number-one reason why young people are saying no to meat.
Stacy Dorris of Chicago became vegetarian when she was 14,

after learning of the conditions for animals on today's farms. "It was pretty easy to change. If you know about what's going on, it just seems cruel to keep eating meat."

Some people give another good reason to pass up the hamburgers and choose veggie burgers instead. "A vegetarian diet is a lot healthier," says Dusty Jacobs, 15, of Tucson, who, along with his 17-year-old brother, Sky, has been a vegetarian all his life. He's right: Vegetarians are less likely to come down with some pretty serious illnesses, like heart disease and some types of cancer. And as a vegetarian, it's really easy to get all of the nutrients that your body needs. (Yes, you *can* get enough protein.)

Some people are vegetarians for what they call human-rights reasons. "The real kicker for me was reading that if just grains and vegetables were grown for humans to eat—instead of cows and animals being raised for food—then everyone in the world could be fed," says Miriam Shakow, 18. Of course, Miriam knows that world hunger is a complicated problem that isn't going to end just because she and some other vegetarians don't eat meat. But she knows that meat production is one piece of the whole world-hunger puzzle.

IT JUST FEELS RIGHT

These are all pretty concrete reasons for going vegetarian, with facts and statistics to back them up. But sometimes, being a vegetarian just feels right.

Many teens have developed very strong personal philosophies against eating meat. Jason Sutton says that when he was 19, something inside just clicked. "I started thinking about it, and I decided that I was not the kind of person who felt comfortable killing animals for food. I felt their death was wrong because it was unnecessary." His friend, 19-year-old Cara Stewart, puts it this way: "I'm a vegetarian for ethical and spiritual reasons. I believe that animals possess a spirit, and they have every right to live and to survive." The choice was clear to her—but not necessarily easy. "It was hard. I grew up eating steak. I love the taste of meat. But I had pets around the house and one day it dawned on me that it just didn't make sense. I couldn't see any difference between a cow and a dog."

Some teens are vegetarians for religious reasons:

- Seventh-Day Adventists (a Christian denomination) grow up believing that a vegetarian diet is what God originally told humans to eat to keep their bodies clean and healthy. By the way, because so many Seventh-Day Adventists are vegetarians, they're a good group of people for health experts to study. And in study after study, Seventh-Day Adventists prove to be healthier than other Americans.

- Many members of Eastern religions, such as Buddhism, Hinduism, and Jainism, are ethical vegetarians. Gautam Shah, a vegetarian college student in Pomona, California, was raised a Jain. He explains: "One of the basic tenets of Jainism is *ahimsa,* which essentially means nonviolence toward other people and other living things. So to kill an animal to eat it would be considered violence by someone who believes in the sanctity of all life."

- People of other religions also recognize that a vegetarian diet is in line with their faiths. Groups such as the Jewish Vegetarians in Baltimore educate people about the aspects of Judaism that support a vegetarian diet. Many Jewish people find that it's easier to keep kosher on a vegetarian diet. And although the Vatican does not promote a meatless diet, some young Catholics also say that a vegetarian diet reflects their own religious values and respect for life.

And finally, here's a really fun reason to be a vegetarian: It can simply make life more interesting. "It's like I've opened up a whole new world of food," says Julie Gerk, 19, of northern California. Julie has discovered grains, beans, and new vegetables and fruits, and she's found vegetarian cookbooks to help her put everything together. Now that she's looking for more than burgers and fries, she notices new options everywhere. "Yesterday I went to an Indian restaurant. And I've discovered other foods like falafel, hummus, and black-bean bisque." Besides introducing her to good food, a vegetarian diet simply makes Julie *feel* good. "I'm taking part in something I believe in. It feels great to be eating with awareness."

CAN ONE PERSON MAKE A DIFFERENCE?

Okay. So maybe these reasons all sound well and good, but you still have your doubts. After all, you're just one person. Everywhere you look, you see people who continue to eat meat. What good can *you* do simply by changing your diet?

Well, many teens think that one person *can* make a difference. "A lot of people say that eating meat is embedded in our system, and that there's nothing I can do by changing my diet," says 19-year-old Holly Friel. "Your being a vegetarian might not change the *whole* world, but it will affect everyone in *your* world. I've even noticed changes in my own family. My grandmother now goes out of her way to try to make things that I can eat. She still eats dead animals in front of me, and it grosses me out, but I have influenced her enough that she has changed some of her habits for me." As one teen puts it, "Every day when you sit down to eat, you're influencing everybody around you. Undoubtedly you're going to cause many people to think about it." Sometimes the effect you have will be obvious, says Samantha. "Three of my friends have become vegetarians because of me."

Even if you're the only vegetarian in your town, you're really not going it alone. "You may feel like just an individual who is doing it," says Samantha, "but really you're a part of a large, caring, compassionate group." Fourteen-year-old Erin figures it this way: "For me, being a vegetarian is like voting—voting against the way animals are kept and slaughtered. People say one vote won't make a difference, but every little bit helps." So, look at the big picture, says Jade: "If you're a vegetarian, and one person over there is a vegetarian, and another person over there is too, it all adds up. The whole collective effort is what makes a difference."

HOW ON EARTH DO YOU GO VEGETARIAN?

What's black and white and read by vegetarian teens all over the country? How On Earth!, *a newsletter that's written especially for young people like you who want to say no to meat. It's not only written for teens, it's written by teens— teens who support "compassionate, ecologically sound living." That means they write cool, straightforward articles about everything from how to convince your parents to let you be a vegetarian to how to start a student group (vegetarian, animal rights, or whatever) at your school. Each issue contains a nutrition question-and-answer column written by a registered dietitian; a boycott update that tells you what companies test their products on animals; yummy meatless recipes; reviews of books and new vegetarian products; a calendar of vegetarian events; plus great articles on health, the environment, and ethics. You'll also get to read letters and poems written by teens around the country.*

How On Earth! *is published by the Vegetarian Education Network (VE-Net). Sally Clinton, VE-Net director, says she wanted to provide fun, informative reading for young vegetarians. Readers tell her that thanks to* How On Earth! *they no longer feel alone. "I hear from people all the time who say, 'I never knew there were so many people out there who think like me.'"*

To receive the newsletter or to contribute to it, contact HOE!, *c/o VE-Net, P.O. Box 3347, West Chester, PA 19381; (717) 529-8638.*

THE FEMINIST DIMENSION

When Esther Brienes was 10, she became a vegetarian for a pretty straightforward reason—out of concern for the animals. But over the years, as she became more and more interested in women's rights, she began to consider another dimension of her diet. "I became more aware of the feminist reasons behind vegetarianism, and suddenly it all seemed to fit together," says Esther, now 18. What "feminist reasons"? What's Esther talking about?

Although pushing a vegetarian diet isn't a top priority of most women's organizations, many feminists believe that there is some connection between their movement and vegetarianism. For one thing, they see both women and animals as having been oppressed for thousands of years. Many feminists also believe that eating meat contributes to starvation around the world—mostly of women and children. Finally, some feminists declare that what they are striving for is a fairer deal not just for women in this world, but for all forms of life. "We see feminism as a very large worldview," says Selma Miriam, co-owner of the Bloodroot Collective, a feminist vegetarian restaurant in Bridgeport, Connecticut. "Our set of values is one that cares about the environment, about all creatures. Unless we push for what's fair and good for everybody, it doesn't matter." To learn more about the feminist-vegetarian connection, you can read The Sexual Politics of Meat *by Carol Adams (New York: Continuum Publishing, 1991). Also, check out the readings and recipes in* The Perennial Political Palate:

The Third Feminist Vegetarian Cookbook *(The Bloodroot Collective, Sanguinaria Publishing, 85 Ferris St., Bridgeport, CT 06605).*

THOSE FAMOUS, FABULOUS VEGGIES

Many a celebrity and historical figure has just said no to meat. According to Vegetarian Times *magazine, here's some of the current crop of hip and happenin' folks who have gone the veggie route:*

TV AND MOVIE STARS: *Rosanna Arquette, Bob Barker, Kim Basinger, Meredith Baxter, Christie Brinkley, Kirk Cameron, Elvira, Sara Gilbert, Bobcat Goldthwait, Dustin Hoffman, Kevin Nealon, Martha Plimpton, Phylicia Rashad, Fred Rogers (yes, that's Mr. Rogers), John Tesh, Cicely Tyson, Lindsay Wagner, Vanessa Williams.* Presumed to be vegetarian but unconfirmed: *Christina Applegate, Lisa Bonet, Cher, Chevy Chase, John Cleese, Bill Cosby, Tom Cruise, Shannen Doherty, Emilio Estevez, Whoopi Goldberg, Anthony Hopkins, Demi Moore, Paul Newman, Jason Priestley.* Nearly vegetarian: *Alec Baldwin, Candice Bergen, Darryl Hannah.*

MUSICIANS: *Joan Armatrading, B-52's vocalist Fred Schneider, Boy George, David Bowie, Kate Bush, Dave and Ray Davies, Def Leppard guitarists Phil Collen and Joe Elliott, Melissa Etheridge, Grateful Dead musicians Jerry Garcia and Phil Lesh, Peter Gabriel, Richie Havens, Indigo Girls vo-*

calist Amy Ray, Michael Jackson, k. d. lang, KRS-ONE, Annie Lennox, Mary's Danish vocalist Julie Ritter, Paul and Linda McCartney, Natalie Merchant, Morrissey, Stevie Nicks, Pearl Jam vocalist Eddie Vedder, Raffi, Red Hot Chili Peppers vocalist Anthony Kiedis, Grace Slick, Michael Stipe, Steve Vai, Ahmet Zappa. Presumed to be vegetarian but unconfirmed: *Paula Abdul, Laurie Anderson, Joan Baez, Jackson Browne, Tracy Chapman, Chubby Checker, Eric Clapton, Elvis Costello, John Denver, Donovan, Bob Dylan, Peter Frampton, David Gilmour, George Harrison, Mickey Hart, Michael Hedges, Bruce Hornsby, Mick Jagger, Elton John, Mark Knopfler, Cyndi Lauper, Julian Lennon, Branford Marsalis, Wynton Marsalis, John Mellencamp, Joni Mitchell, Van Morrison, Tom Petty, Robert Plant, ♀ (the artist formerly known as Prince), Bonnie Raitt, Michelle Shocked, Bruce Springsteen, Ringo Starr, James Taylor, Mary Travers, Suzanne Vega, Tom Waits, Neil Young.* Nearly vegetarian: *Kenny G, Arlo Guthrie, Billy Idol, Lenny Kravitz, U2 guitarist Edge.*

ATHLETIC TYPES: *Hank Aaron (baseball home-run champ), Surya Bonaly (Olympic ice-skating silver medalist), Chris Campbell (Olympic bronze-medal wrestler), Estelle Gray and Cheryl Marek (world-record cross-country tandem cyclists), Kathy Johnson (Olympic silver-medal gymnast), Billie Jean King (tennis champion), Killer Kowalski (champion wrestler), Tony*

LaRussa (Oakland A's manager), Marv Levy (Buffalo Bills manager), Carl Lewis (Olympic gold-medal runner and long jumper), Edwin Moses (Olympic gold-medal hurdler), Martina Navratilova (tennis star), Bill Pearl (Mr. Universe and bodybuilder), Dave Scott (six-time Ironman triathlon winner), Debbie Spaeth-Herring (Georgia State power-lifter), Bill Walton (basketball star).

A FEW OTHER FAMOUS FOLKS: Berke Breathed (cartoonist), Henry Heimlich, M.D. (creator of the Heimlich maneuver), Steven Jobs (computer wiz; founded Apple), Casey Kasem (Top 40 countdown radio personality), Colman McCarthy (Washington Post columnist), Dean Ornish, M.D. (cardiologist and author), Sy Sperling (president of the Hair Club for Men).

FAMOUS VEGGIES IN HISTORY: Louisa May Alcott, Clara Barton, Buddha, Cesar Chavez, Leonardo da Vinci, Charles Darwin, Thomas Edison, Albert Einstein, Mahatma Gandhi, Horace Greeley, John Milton, Malcolm Muggeridge, Scott Nearing, Sir Isaac Newton, Ovid, Plato, Alexander Pope, Plutarch, Pythagoras, Jean Jacques Rousseau, Henry Salt, Albert Schweitzer, George Bernard Shaw, Percy Bysshe Shelley, Upton Sinclair, Isaac Bashevis Singer, Socrates, Henry David Thoreau, Leo Tolstoy, Peter Tosh, Voltaire, H. G. Wells.

CHAPTER 2

FOR THE PLANET

"I think it's really messed up that one species—humans—can cause so much damage. Animal-based agriculture is a big part of that."

—*John Lanzerotta, 17*

You arrive at school one morning, still sleepy, to discover that there's a morning assembly—some presentation about the environment. Yawn. It's a little early in the day for yet another lecture from "the experts" about how it's up to *your* generation to save the planet. But when you get to the auditorium, you notice that this assembly is different. For one thing, the people who are making the presentation *are* your generation. It's a group of teens who call themselves YES! (which stands for Youth for Environmental Sanity).

The YES! tour is a group of young activists who travel from high school to high school teaching students across America about important environmental issues. They talk about rain-forest depletion, pollution, and global warming. One topic sometimes catches their audience off guard, says YES! member Jade Thome. "When we talk about how being a vegetarian can help the environment, most people are like, 'Huh?' It's the first time they've heard anything about it. They're like, 'Yeah, right, give me the facts.' We don't push it and try to turn everyone into a vegetarian. But once the facts are presented, people realize that to say that you care about the environment and to keep on eating so much meat is pretty hypocritical."

Just what are the facts? "Meat production contributes to soil erosion, desertification, rain-forest destruction, global warming, and water pollution," says Jade. "And don't forget about the chemicals that are sprayed on the food that animals eat."

That's just the beginning. The raising of any kind of animal for food also uses up energy, water, grain, and land. "Livestock production is the most ecologically damaging component of American agriculture," says Alan Durning, a senior researcher at Worldwatch Institute in Washington, D.C., an organization that researches the facts about global issues. Durning wrote an important paper called *Taking Stock: Animal Farming and the Environment.* Much of the following information comes from his report. (Note: For specific references for facts appearing in this and other chapters, turn to Appendix 2 at the back of the book.)

Meat production uses a lot of land.

● Almost one-half (about 45 percent) of the land in the continental United States is used for meat production. Why so much land? It's needed to grow grain that's fed to the livestock. Which leads us to the fact that . . .

Meat production gobbles up grain.

● Almost 40 percent of the world's grain supply is fed to livestock. In the United States, 70 percent of the grain consumed is fed to animals.

● It takes at least: seven pounds of grain to make one pound of pork; five pounds of grain to make one pound of beef; and three pounds of grain to make one pound of chicken.

By the way, most of the grain fed to animals is perfectly suitable for people. Energy experts say that it would be far more efficient to simply eat the grain, rather than eat the animals that eat the grain. And hunger experts agree: While grain is fed to animals, hundreds of millions of people in this world go hungry. Some estimate that, if all of the world's population were vegetarian, there would be enough food to go around right now. Of course, hunger is a complicated political, social, and economic issue, the solution to which requires much more than a simple shift in diet. Still, the fact that so much grain is necessary to satisfy our taste for meat is food for thought.

It is not a wise development policy for struggling countries to depend on a meat-rich diet, experts say, because it makes countries dependent on imported grain and can widen the gap between rich and poor nations. Right now, countries already in major debt are going even deeper because they need to import grain for meat production.

A vegetarian diet saves water.

- About one-half of the water consumed in the United States goes to livestock production. In the western states, livestock production accounts for more than 70 percent of water consumed.
- It takes about 100 gallons of irrigation water every day to feed one person with meat, milk, and eggs.
- In California, it takes 23 gallons of water to produce 1 pound of tomatoes; 25 gallons of water to produce 1 pound of wheat; 33 gallons of water to produce 1 pound of carrots; and more than 5,200 gallons of water to produce 1 pound of beef. (California beef needs so much water because it's being raised in a desert.)
- On average around the country, it takes about 2,500 gallons of water to produce 1 pound of feedlot beef.
- Much feedlot beef relies on water pumped from the gigantic Ogallala aquifer in the southern plains. Some parts of this water source have already been severely depleted.

A vegetarian diet saves energy (coal, oil, and natural gas).

- The fewer animal products you eat, the more energy you conserve. A vegan diet is the most energy-efficient: It takes more than three times as much fossil-fuel energy to feed a meat eater than it does to feed a person who eats no meat or dairy products.

● It takes the equivalent of about 50 gallons of gasoline to produce a year's worth of red meat and poultry for the typical American.

Meat production creates pollution.

● Livestock farms produce millions of tons of animal wastes. When these wastes reach rivers and lakes, they cause algae to grow and choke out other plants and animals.

● Nitrates from manure pollute groundwater. One-fifth of wells in livestock states such as Iowa, Kansas, and Nebraska have high nitrate levels. Nitrates are linked to cancer and nervous-system problems.

● Gases from manure escape into the air and contribute to acid rain.

Meat production causes topsoil loss. Topsoil is the important layer of soil that holds the nutrients that plants need.

● For every pound of feedlot beef produced, 35 pounds of topsoil erode away.

● It takes 200 to 1,000 years for nature to form one inch of topsoil.

Meat production causes *desertification*, which describes how land that was once productive becomes barren and lifeless.

● Here's how it happens: Cattle overgraze grasses and plants until those grasses and plants die and weeds take over. Weeds don't anchor the soil very well, so the soil erodes away as the area is trampled by hooves, blown by wind, or washed by rain.

- Estimates say that about 70 percent of the world's dry rangeland is at least moderately desertified—including land in the western United States.

A vegetarian diet saves forests.

- More than one-third of the forests of Central America have been cleared since 1960, mostly to raise cattle for beef. In Latin America, forests are cleared primarily for pasture. Nepal has lost an estimated one-half its Himalayan forests in the past 20 years, partly for fodder (food) for livestock.

- As forests are lost, so are species. Tropical forests cover just 7 percent of the earth but contain perhaps half of its species. If the Amazon basin continues to be deforested at the same rate as it was in the 1980s, 15 percent of all plant species may be lost by the year 2000.

- Clearing forests increases the amount of carbon dioxide in the atmosphere. Carbon dioxide is called a greenhouse gas because it traps the heat of the sun and contributes to global warming. (Cows and manure give off methane, another greenhouse gas.)

- Cattle grazing threatens forests in the United States, too. About one-half of the forest land here is used for livestock grazing. Although trees are left standing, the cattle destroy grasses and small plants, affecting the entire forest ecosystem.

John, 17, of Massachusetts, says he's been seeing more and more articles about meat production in the environmental books and magazines he reads. And he's glad: "I feel like it's important. If you consider yourself an environmentalist, you should get off of animal agriculture."

WHAT YOU CAN DO

- If the issues just discussed are important to you, you can reduce the amount of meat you eat. The Beyond Beef campaign in Washington, D.C., teaches that cutting beef consumption in half (and replacing it with plant foods, not other meat) can greatly help the environment. Some environmentalists say Americans should cut back even more than that, like down to about one-quarter of what we now eat, or less.

- Take a closer look at your next meal: What kind of resources were used to produce it? What pollution was caused? Were chemical pesticides used? What waste was involved in packaging the products? How was the food transported from the farm to the store to your table? Besides cutting back on the amount of meat you eat, you might:

  1. Shop for organic, locally grown produce. (Check out a farmers' market.)
  2. Avoid products with excess packaging. (Check out the bulk section of your store.)

- Read more about how meat production affects the environment. Start with these books:

  Diet for a Small Planet by Frances Moore Lappé. The book that first uncovered how our food choices affect the world around us.

Diet for a New America by John Robbins. Reveals the real costs behind humans' dependence on animal products.

Beyond Beef by Jeremy Rifkin. Tells how cattle and beef became such a big part of our society in the first place.

● Write to EarthSave for a copy of the booklet *Our Food Our World,* which includes more facts about how meat affects our planet. (Your classmates and teachers might be interested in seeing it, too.) Write P.O. Box 68, Santa Cruz, CA 95063-0068.

● Write your national representatives and encourage them to support legislation that promotes a healthier planet. Be specific. Things to encourage: better management of western rangeland and government support for organic fruit and vegetable farmers. (The government spends lots of money helping livestock farmers and feed growers; why not the same support for growers of organic fruits and veggies?) Write U.S. House of Representatives, Washington, DC 20515; U.S. Senate, Washington, DC 20510.

HEY! THERE ARE CATTLE AT MY CAMPSITE! *Did you know that cattle are allowed to graze in national parks and on other public lands? Cattle ranchers like to graze their herds there because the U.S. government charges a much cheaper grazing fee than private landowners do. (They even get tax money to build fences and things.) Public-lands grazing is a big problem in the West, where 70 percent of all land is used for livestock grazing. Grazing seriously degrades the* land and threatens other species, including prairie dogs, grizzly bears, coyotes, and wolves. Many environmentalists are encouraging the government to change its grazing fees and policies. For more information, contact the Ranching Task Force, P.O. Box 5784, Tucson, AZ 85703, or Rose Strickland, Sierra Club, P.O. Box 8409, Reno, NV 89507.

NO FISH STORY

True, nobody's chopping down forests to clear pasture for trout and salmon. But fishing and fish farming, or aquaculture, cause their own environmental problems. For one thing, the Earth's waters are terribly overfished. Experts say we've just about reached the limit of how many fish we can regularly take from the ocean without depleting the stock. Also, nets used in fishing sometimes accidentally kill animals other than those that are being fished, including dolphins, seals, and even whales. And on fish farms, many fish are packed into small spaces, upsetting the ecological balance all around them.

YES! SAYS YES, YOU CAN MAKE A DIFFERENCE

A few years ago, Ocean Robbins (son of Diet for a New America author John Robbins) identified a problem: "I looked at high schools around the country and I saw a lot of young people who feel very concerned about the state of the planet and don't really feel that they can do anything to improve it. I wanted to change that." So he and his buddy Ryan Eliason founded YES! or Youth for

Environmental Sanity. "One of the best parts of YES! is that it's entirely youth-organized," notes Ryan. "We're setting an example. We're saying that youth can change the world." The YES! tour visits more than 300 high schools each year, teaching students about animal agriculture, deforestation, pollution, toxic wastes, and other global issues. But they don't just gripe about the problems and then leave you wondering what to do: They offer workshops, teach you how to start your own environmental club, and even give advice on working with your community leaders. For the serious planet-saver, YES! offers summer training camps and a youth action guide featuring more tips for getting involved.

YES! is made up of about 15 multi-ethnic youth representatives from the United States, Canada, and Mexico. Says Ocean: "One of our goals is to encourage teens of all nationalities, races, and religions to get involved. The environment is one thing we can all share." You can book YES! at your school: Contact the YES! Tour, 706 Frederick St., Santa Cruz, CA 95062 or call (408) 459-9344.

YOU CAN SPREAD THE MESSAGE AT YOUR SCHOOL

More than 80 percent of teenagers say that it's "in" to care about the environment, according to the trend-tracking company Teenage Research Unlimited. But many high school environmentalists want to make sure that caring about the *environment and vegetarianism are more than just passing trends. They're teaching their peers about the facts behind the fad:*

Fernando Delgado and Rachel Seed presented a workshop on vegetarianism at an environmental conference sponsored by their high school, Niles West, near Chicago. They taught how meat production affects the planet, animals, and the health of people who eat it. The most challenging part? "Working together and trying to memorize everything," says Rachel. The team also presented its workshop at an international youth conference in Colorado. Their hard work paid off: "At one of the talks, everyone was interested, and people came up afterward and said they loved it," says Fernando. Adds Rachel: "Twenty people gave me their phone numbers and said, 'You're going to have to call me and give me more information.' I think it did persuade some of them to become vegetarian."

Ever heard of an environmental slumber party? Phil Radford, a student leader of the environmental club at Oak Park–River Forest High School in Illinois organized one. At an overnight teach-in, students learned all about the topic "How Our Food Choices Affect the Environment." Workshops ran late into the night. How'd Phil choose the subject? "I wanted it to be something people could relate to, not some abstract thing. I didn't want to get up there and say,

'Okay, everybody, this is global warming.' I
thought it would be a good idea to talk about
something that people feel they can do something about in their everyday lives."

CHAPTER 3

FOR THE ANIMALS

❝I did not become a vegetarian for my health. I did it for the health of the chickens.❞

—Isaac Bashevis Singer

While the environmental rap about a vegetarian diet makes a lot of sense, many young vegetarians will tell you that they're doing it for a different reason: for the animals. Says Michelle Shook, 18, of Ontario: "My vegetarianism all started out because I love animals. The environmental and health reasons are just bonuses."

David Berman, 18, became a vegetarian when he was in eighth grade. "I just started feeling really guilty about eating meat after I had learned about the cruelty involved in the way animals are raised. It was hard, because all of my favorite foods were meat—like hamburgers and chicken—and I didn't really even like vegetables." But the more David read about how farm animals are raised, the more he wanted to stick to his decision. In high school, he started up his own animal-rights group, called S.P. A.R.E. (it stands for Students Protecting Animals' Rights & the Environment), and one thing S.P. A.R.E. taught was that being a vegetarian is one way to take a stand against animal cruelty.

What's all this talk about animal cruelty? You can't exactly see it just by looking at the meat in your supermarket. We all grow up thinking of the plastic-wrapped steaks and chicken wings in the same way we think about any other food—they're just *food.* "It sort of erases people's compassion," says Michelle, "because you can't even tell that what you're buying is from an animal." If we do stop at all to think about where the food came from, we usually picture a peaceful little barnyard scene. "People think it's like this happy farmer wearing overalls, and all of the animals running around the farm, and hamburgers growing on cornstalks," says Danny Seo, 16. "But it's just not like that."

What *is* it like? About 15 years ago, authors Jim Mason and Peter Singer wrote a book about what today's farms look like from the inside. They called their book *Animal Factories* because they found that animals are raised in settings much more like high-tech factories than farms. Let's take a look:

SOME BASIC FACTS OF THE FACTORY FARM

- Every year in this country, more than six billion animals are slaughtered for food.

- About 90 percent of the animals that people eat in the United States are raised in confinement. This means that animals are crowded into pens and cages that are too small for them. Many animals spend their entire lives indoors in dark, filthy buildings.

- Factory farms are just that—*factories*. Farm chores that the farmer once performed, such as feeding and cleaning, are now done by machines. In an egg-laying factory, for instance, a conveyor belt carries food to birds in their cages, and another conveyor belt carries away eggs.

- Factory farmers try to make animals grow faster by feeding them things like antibiotics and hormones.

- Animals endure long trips from the factory farm to the slaughterhouse, riding on crowded trucks. The trip often leaves them sick, injured, hungry, or disoriented.

- At the slaughterhouse, animals are *supposed* to be protected by something called the Humane Slaughter Act. This act, in part, says that an animal is supposed to be unconscious before it is killed. But there are many loopholes to this act. For one thing, the act doesn't even consider chickens, turkeys, and other birds to be animals, and therefore doesn't apply to them. Because most farm animals are poultry, this means that most farm animals today are fully conscious while they are being killed. And there's very little inspection to make sure that animals that *are* covered by the act are killed humanely.

Facts like these have gotten teens thinking. "People need to be informed," says Erin Martinez, 14, of El Paso, Texas. "The meat industry doesn't want people to know how it really is. I mean, their slogans like 'Beef: It's what's for dinner' sound great and everything. Or you'll see a picture of a smiling cow on a milk carton. But they're giving an inaccurate picture of what it's like."

CHECK OUT THESE CHICKENS

- A single egg-laying factory may contain hundreds of thousands of birds. Birds who lay eggs are crammed into small cages with so many other birds that they barely have room to turn around—about half a square foot of space per bird. Birds produced just for meat (broilers) aren't caged, but are just as crowded on the floors of buildings. To prevent crowded, stressed birds from pecking each other to death, farmers debeak them, using a hot blade.
- In the egg industry, male chicks are considered useless because they won't lay eggs when they grow up. Soon after hatching, they are gassed, tossed in plastic bags to suffocate, or ground alive for animal feed.
- "Free-range" eggs don't necessarily come from birds living in the great outdoors; most "free-range" birds are kept indoors, just not caged. Free-range chickens, like other egg-layers, are also eventually slaughtered.
- Turkeys are raised under conditions similar to those for chickens.

If all the chickens that are factory-farmed for American dinner tables each year were laid out beak to toe, they would form a line reaching to the moon and back twice, says the book *Animal Factories.* Even some people who don't eat red meat don't mind eating chickens. Why? "It seems to me like people have more sympathy for animals that are more like our domesticated animals," says Erin. "Like with a cow, you can pet it and look into its sad-looking eyes. People think chickens are just mean, dirty animals anyway." The way Danny Seo figures, people simply care more about animals that they think are intelligent. "People think chickens are stupid."

THE MAKIN' OF BACON

- Pig farmers raise mainly female pigs, or sows, because sows produce "crops" of piglets. These sows go from one pregnancy to the next without a break, and farmers sometimes inject pigs with hormones to make them produce more piglets quickly and inexpensively. A sow gives birth and feeds her piglets in a very small stall—with no room for her to walk or turn around.

- Pigs are usually calm and friendly, but confined pigs will bite each other's tails. Farmers prevent this by removing the tails and some of the teeth of newborn pigs. They also notch the pigs' ears to tell them apart. Pigs develop foot, ankle, and leg problems from standing on concrete floors, and many suffer lung damage and pneumonia from ammonia and other toxic gases that accumulate in their buildings.

No one can blame a farmer for wanting a large crop. But some teens say it seems odd to think of animals as "crops" in the first place. "I think it's wrong for pigs and chickens and cows to be treated like products," says Miriam Shakow, 18. Eighteen-year-old Tabatha Bruce agrees. As an animal care-taker intern at the Farm Sanctuary, a shelter for former factory-farm animals, Tabatha had the opportunity to get to know some farm animals first-hand. Some of Tabatha's pals included Marcia the rooster, Frankie the broiler chicken, and Chelsea the sheep. "It was great to get to know the personalities of the animals," she says. "Each one is an individual. It's so different to look at them that way. Not as products. Without dollar signs attached."

HOW NOW, BROWN COW

- Cattle generally spend more time outdoors than other factory-farmed animals, but they spend their last months confined on a feedlot, getting fattened up for market. Feedlot cattle are branded, castrated, and de-horned without anesthetics.

- Cows are moved from pasture to feedlot and then to slaughterhouse on crowded metal trucks. Sometimes a cow falls or becomes injured and can't move with the other animals. These cows are called "downers" and are sometimes prodded, dragged with chains, or simply abandoned, with no food or water, to die. There's no gov-ernment policy ensuring that injured animals are treated compassionately. Most downed animals are processed for humans to eat, even though eating sick animals can cause health problems in people.

- In order for dairy cows to produce milk continuously, they must give birth every year. A mother's calf is taken away from her when it is just a few days old, so that it doesn't drink her milk.

- Dairy cows are forced to produce 10 times the amount of milk they would naturally produce and are milked by machine two or three times a day. All of these milkings leave most dairy cows with swollen, diseased udders. A new substance called bovine growth hormone, or BGH, is now used to boost milk production even more (despite the fact that there's already a surplus of milk in this country). When a dairy cow's milk-producing career is over, she is slaughtered for meat.

Adults often cut back on red meat and high-fat dairy products because they want to be healthy. Young people say that it's just as logical to give up these products out of concern for the animals themselves. Says Miriam, "I see the mistreatment of animals as a *very* concrete reason for being vegetarian. I don't want to contribute to the industry in any way." She has particular feelings about dairy: "I learned that humans are the only mammals that continue to drink milk after nursing—and the milk we drink is that of other animals. It seems reasonable to me that people aren't really meant to eat dairy products."

THE VEAL ORDEAL

- Veal calves come from dairy cows. Every year, one million newly born calves are taken from their mothers soon after birth.
- Veal calves are kept in narrow wooden crates and chained at the neck, allowing them no space to turn

around or lie down comfortably. They aren't allowed to get exercise, because exercise would cause their muscles to develop and toughen.

● Calves are fed an iron-deficient "milk replacer" gruel to keep their flesh white. It also makes the calves anemic. Some become so anemic that they die before getting to slaughter.

Even many people who aren't vegetarians think veal is pretty bad news. "I don't know *anyone* my age who eats it," says Anna Balla, 19.

SOMETHING'S FISHY

"But you eat fish, don't you?" That's what people will ask you when you tell them you're a vegetarian. That's strange, says Michelle Shook: "I don't consider fish vegetables." When Erin Martinez became a vegetarian, she stopped eating fish *first*. "I know that's odd, because most people do it just the opposite. But I've always been fascinated by fish. I had a pet fish, so fish are almost like dogs to me. I realized that eating fish was like eating my pet."

Here's the scoop: A fish has a central nervous system, so it's able to feel pain and trauma when it's hooked or netted. Fish get oxygen from water, so removing them from water suffocates them. Fish are mass-farmed in factory-like settings, too. Fish farms are like floating cages, filled with perhaps hundreds of thousands of fish. Many farmed fish become sick and die in captivity.

Still, many people don't think of fish as sensitive creatures, notes Erin. "People don't see fish in the same way because fish are from a completely different world. They don't have fur, they don't walk—they're just completely different."

WHAT YOU CAN DO

- Educate yourself! To learn more about factory farming, read *Animal Factories* by Jim Mason and Peter Singer (Harmony Books). You can use it for a book report or a term paper.

- Learn together. Invite friends over to watch the video *Food Without Fear.* It's a good video because it deals with a disturbing topic—the dark side of meat production— in a powerful and entertaining way. You can rent it from the North American Vegetarian Society, P.O. Box 72, Dolgeville, NY 13329.

- Learn about other sources of animal cruelty as well. Did you know that many cosmetic companies still perform painful product-safety tests on animals, even though other more reliable and more humane testing methods exist? Toys and household and office products are tested on animals, too. For a list of companies that don't test on animals and those that do, write to People for the Ethical Treatment of Animals, P.O. Box 42516, Washington, DC 20015. Also, the *How On Earth!* newsletter contains a regular "Boycott Report," which will update you on the animal-testing policies of various companies. Write to *HOE!* at P.O. Box 3347, West Chester, PA 19381.

- Take a hard look at serious animal issues and form your own opinion. How do you feel, for instance, about vivisection (the process of using living animals for research) in laboratories, or dissection in science class? Read about these topics to learn the facts. A good place to start is the book *Animals in Society* by Zoe Weil; it was written especially for students. To order, call Animalearn at (215) 887-0816. For ideas about what you can do to change things, read *Kids Can Save the Animals: 101 Easy Things to Do,* by Ingrid Newkirk, director of People for the Ethical Treatment of Animals (New York: Warner Books, 1989).

● Empower yourself! There's nothing like meeting other like-minded people to give your spirit and commitment a boost. At the Youth Empowerment Workshops (sponsored by the Vegetarian Education Network and Animalearn), you'll find other teens who care about animals, vegetarianism, and the environment. Says one workshop participant: "Being with twenty other people made me feel like I wasn't alone, like my cause was worthwhile." Contact VE-Net at P.O. Box 3347, West Chester, PA 19381; or Animalearn at 801 Old York Road, #204, Jenkintown, PA 19046-1685.

● Speak out! Write your national representatives and encourage them to support legislation that promotes humane treatment of animals on the farm and everywhere. Write U.S. House of Representatives, Washington, DC 20515; U.S. Senate, Washington, DC 20510.

THEY'RE ANIMAL ADVOCATES!

Feeling alone in your feelings about animals? Meet these folks who also care:

● *Laurel Wilson, 15: Laurel's worked hard to help the animals. She attends demonstrations about animal issues and was a local coordinator in a campaign to get vegetarian options in local fast-food restaurants. She's even been interviewed on a radio talk show. "I do a lot of things to show that teenagers can do just as much as adults can," says Laurel.*

● *Danny Seo, 16: Danny is definitely a doer. He started an animal rights/environmental group called Earth 2000 in his hometown of Reading, Pennsylvania. He even organized a big demonstration at the Danish embassy in Washington, D.C., to protest brutal whaling methods in Denmark. He sees vegetarianism as a natural part of his compassion and efforts for animals. "There's a lot of cruelty in the meat industry. Being a vegetarian is the ethically correct thing to do."*

● *Marc Freligh, 15: Marc also started a group, called Students for Animal Protection. Marc's group established some vegetarian days in his school cafeteria and served a vegetarian meal to schoolteachers in honor of the Great American Meatout (March 20). His goal: "To get a meatless option on the school menu every day." Both Marc and Danny received the 1993 AAVS Student Animal Advocate Award for their outstanding work (AAVS stands for American Anti-Vivisection Society. See Appendix 1 for more information.)*

WHAT DO THEY MEAN BY "ANIMAL RIGHTS"? *Simply put, "animal rights" describes the belief that all species have the right not to be exploited or killed just to satisfy the whims and desires of people. Do you have a pet dog or cat that you love and provide with food, shelter, and a nice* *place to sleep? People who support animal rights think that all animals, not just our pets, deserve compassion. They believe that animals aren't the property of humans and that they shouldn't be used to serve people or to make money. They note that animals can be sensitive, intelligent creatures who feel pain and fear, and they think that animals should be protected from all senseless suffering—whether it's at a fur farm, a research lab, a zoo or a circus, or on a factory farm.*

Animal-rights activists often get a bad rap. Many people think that they're all wild "radicals" who are more interested in saving a cow or pig than in the well-being of humans. "Animal-rights people usually help people, too," says Zoe Weil, director of Animalearn, a nonprofit education group for young people. "And if someone is trying to make the world better, that's terrific!"

MARK YOUR CALENDAR!		
	March 20	*Great American Meatout*
	Mother's Day	*National Veal Ban Action*
	October 1	*World Vegetarian Day*
	October 2	*World Farm Animals Day*

For info on how you can observe these days, contact the Farm Animal Reform Movement at (800)-MEATOUT or the North American Vegetarian Society at (518) 568-7970.

CHAPTER 4

FOR YOUR HEALTH

*❝I don't understand why asking people to eat a well-balanced
vegetarian diet is considered drastic, while it is medically
conservative to cut people open or put them on powerful
cholesterol-lowering drugs for the rest of their lives.❞*

—Dean Ornish, M.D.

~~~~~~~~~~We've talked about how a vegetarian diet can be good for the environment and good for the animals. Now it's time to look at why a vegetarian diet is good for *you*, too.

Hey, wait! Don't turn the page. You're probably tempted to skip over this health stuff. But even if you don't care about health, your parents most likely do, and you're going to have to convince them that, as a vegetarian, you're not going to shrivel up and die.

Even though adults become vegetarians for health reasons, they sometimes think that it's unhealthy for young people to do so. "A lot of parents are concerned," says David, 18. "A lot of them have misunderstandings about the diet." Parents will insist that you *need* to eat meat because you're still growing. In all fairness, it's understandable why they freak out about it. When they were growing up, there wasn't nearly as much scientific research on vegetarian diets as there is now. Years ago, the only stories that made it into the newspapers were scary articles about sickly, scrawny kids who were taken from their parents after it was discovered that they were being fed a "vegetarian diet" of nothing but sprouts and dry toast. What parent wouldn't be concerned? Fortunately, the truth is that this kind of horror story has absolutely nothing to do with the way that real vegetarians eat.

Today there's a ton of proof that a vegetarian diet can be perfectly healthy for both adults *and* teens. This chapter contains some things that your parents (and you) will be happy to know. (Note: If they need more convincing, show them the scientific references for this chapter, in Appendix 2.)

THE EXPERTS SAY VEGETARIANS ARE A-OK

The Most Respected Nutrition Experts Say a Vegetarian Diet Is Healthy for Teens

The official 1993 position paper of the American Dietetic Association (ADA) says flat-out that a vegetarian diet is a "healthful and nutritionally adequate" way to eat. The ADA says that vegetarian diets—even vegan diets that include no milk products or eggs—can be perfectly appropriate for all age groups, including children and teens.

In 1991, the ADA created a special group, the Vegetarian Nutrition Dietetic Practice Group, for dietitians who want to teach people about the benefits of a vegetarian diet. Within just two years, the group included 1,400 enthusiastic health professionals wanting to provide quality nutrition care to the growing vegetarian population.

Vegetarian Kids Grow Just Fine

Your parents might worry that a vegetarian diet will stunt your growth. But unless they catch you eating only berries and bran, they needn't worry. Study after study shows that vegetarian children reach the right height and weight for their ages and that they grow at a healthy rate. A study of more than 400 young children in Tennessee showed that kids can grow up big and strong even without dairy products and eggs. The key to being a healthy vegetarian: eating a variety of foods and getting plenty of calories to grow on.

Vegetarian Teens May Be More in Line with Current Dietary Guidelines Than Nonvegetarian Teens

The latest dietary guidelines (like the ones in the Food Guide Pyramid, our government's official illustration showing how much of what foods you should be eating each day) say that we should get plenty of fruit, veggies, and grains, and that we should cut back on fatty, salty, and sugary foods. And guess what? Researchers have noted that some young vegetarians eat more of the good foods that they're supposed to and fewer of the junky foods they're not. All sorts of health experts have said that we should eat this way—everyone from the U.S. Surgeon General to the American Cancer Society. These sources haven't exactly come right out and said "Be a vegetarian," but they've come pretty close.

There's a Mountain of Evidence Showing How Healthy a Vegetarian Diet Is

The largest nutrition study ever (the China Project on Nutrition, Health, and the Environment) showed that rural Chinese people who eat a mostly vegetarian diet are healthier than those who eat lots of meat and dairy. Researcher T. Colin Campbell of Cornell University says, "I think in the next five to ten years, we'll have evidence [showing that vegetarianism is the healthiest diet] that is as strong as, let's say, the evidence that cigarette smoking causes lung cancer." There's already so much great vegetarian research that health experts routinely get together at big meetings to share their findings. In 1992, more than 400 people from 30 countries attended the Second International Congress on Vegetarian Nutrition in Washington, D.C. Their conclusion: Both vegetarian adults and children are generally well-nourished people who enjoy lower rates of serious illness.

VEGETARIANS ARE HEALTHIER, AND WE'RE NOT JUST TALKING COLDS AND FLU

Vegetarians Have Much Less Heart Disease Than People Who Eat Meat

Heart disease is the leading cause of death in the United States. But does it have to be? One study of 25,000 people showed that men who ate meat every day had three times the risk of dying from a heart attack than men who ate no meat. Another study suggests that an ovo-lacto vegetarian's chance of getting heart disease is 24 percent lower than that of a meat eater, and a vegan's chance is 57 percent lower. Dr. Dean Ornish of the University of California, San Francisco, discovered that a vegetarian diet, along with exercise and meditation, can even begin unclogging blocked arteries in heart-disease patients. And many vegetarians have lower cholesterol levels than nonvegetarians. (Vegetarians also have lower blood pressure.)

Why is a vegetarian diet so heart-healthy? Well, it usually contains much less saturated fat and cholesterol, two things that contribute to heart disease. (Saturated fat is found mostly in animal products, and cholesterol is found *only* in animal products, so a vegan diet is completely cholesterol-free.) By the way, heart disease isn't just an old person's worry: Doctors have found evidence of heart disease in people as young as age 15.

Vegetarians Are Less Likely to Get Certain Types of Cancer

It's hard to believe that something as simple as changing what you eat can help protect against cancer, but experts say it's true. The National Cancer Institute says that two out of three cancers are related to our diets. Vegetarians really come out ahead: One study showed that the rate of deaths from cancer among Seventh-Day Adventists, a largely vegetarian group, is about one-half that of the rest of the population. People who eat a lot of meat have a higher risk of colon cancer. Also, breast cancer is much less common in countries where women eat low-fat vegetarian diets. No one knows exactly why vegetarians have less cancer. Researchers say it could have to do with the fact that vegetarians eat more fruits, vegetables, and grains—and less fat—than meat eaters do; these factors may help strengthen the body's immune system.

Vegetarians Have a Lower Risk for Other Types of Illness, Too

The list of health advantages goes on and on: In general, vegetarians are less obese than nonvegetarians, have lower blood pressure and a lower risk for kidney stones, gallstones, and diabetes. Some studies suggest that vegetarians may also have less osteoporosis, a condition common among older women, in which their bones lose matter, become weak, and fracture easily. Osteoporosis is a complicated issue, and bone docs aren't sure why some people get it and others don't; lots of things, including heredity, are believed to play a part. Where diet is concerned, you might think that people living in countries where they don't eat much dairy would be the ones with all the osteoporosis. But osteoporosis is actually most common in Western countries, like the United States, where people eat lots of dairy products and get lots of calcium. And experts have noted that countries consuming the most animal protein in general have the highest rates of the disease.

HOW A VEGGIE DIET MIGHT HELP YOU FEEL BETTER TODAY

Feeling Sluggish?

It's right before math class, and you can't even keep your eyes open, let alone add and subtract. Some people who switch to a meatless diet say they feel more alert and vigorous and less fatigued. Of course, it depends on what you eat. Some teens who simply drop the meat and live on vegetarian junk food say they feel absolutely *exhausted*. Fatigue has many causes, not just diet. But some people find they can boost their energy with a diet full of grains, fresh fruits and vegetables, and dishes made with cooked beans.

Trying to Shed a Few Pounds?

The latest word on weight loss is that a low-fat, vegetarian diet is a great way to slim down. Why? According to weight-loss experts, it's not always *how much* you eat, but also *what kind* of food you eat that matters. Many people are overweight because they eat too much fat, not too much food. Typically, the foods to choose for weight loss are complex carbohydrates (pasta, grains, beans, potatoes, and other veggies) and the ones to avoid are fatty foods (fatty meats and dairy products, plus fatty plant foods such as oil, nuts, and avocados). Most people find they can eat a *lot* of food on a veggie diet and still stay slim. It's no wonder that vegetarians are generally leaner than nonvegetarians.

Training for the Team?

All kinds of top-notch athletes are vegetarians, from Dave Scott, six-time winner of the Ironman triathlon, to tennis star Martina Navratilova. These athletes know that a diet loaded with complex carbohydrates provides the best fuel for endurance and strength. Sports nutritionists say it's a myth that you need to eat a huge amount of excess protein to build muscles. So you can skip the protein shakes and bacon-and-egg breakfasts and fuel up instead on vegetarian fare such as breads, cereals, pasta, rice, beans, and veggies.

Want to Ease Those Cramps?

Some girls find that a vegetarian diet helps ease painful menstrual cramps. Dairy products, red meat, and poultry contain the type of dietary fat that the body uses to produce something called series-two prostaglandins—hormone-like chemicals that are known to trigger muscle contraction and other responses that can make cramps worse. You can read more about this in a book called *Menstrual Cramps: A Self-Help Program,* by Susan Lark, M.D. (Los Altos, CA: Westchester Publishing Company, 1993). Another period plus: Studies have found that vegetarian girls get their first menstrual period (called menarche) later than nonvegetarians. Research indicates that girls who have a later age of menarche often have a lower risk of several kinds of cancers, including breast cancer.

Is Pizza Face a Problem?

There's no magic diet to get rid of zits, but some doctors say that a low-fat, vegetarian diet may be helpful. As described above, animal fats are linked to prostaglandins, which also stimulate inflammation (heat, redness, swelling, and pain)—something you'd want to avoid if you're trying to prevent acne.

THE HEALTH MYTHS ABOUT VEGETARIANISM (AND WHY THEY'RE WRONG)

Myth #1: You Can't Get Enough Protein

Actually, getting too little protein is almost never a problem for people. Most meat-eating Americans get way too *much* protein. And even vegetarians get more protein than they really need. There's evidence that getting too much protein may be linked to health problems such as cancer and osteoporosis.

You can also easily get all the protein you need from plant foods; some vegetarians get protein from eggs or dairy, too. If you've heard that vegetarians must combine foods in all sorts of complicated ways to get "complete" protein, forget it. Research shows that you don't have to put foods together in a certain way to get good protein. You can get all the protein you need just by eating a variety of foods every day.

Myth #2: Vegetarians Can't Get Enough Iron

Again, untrue. Vegetarian teens do not have more iron-deficiency anemia than other teens. Meat isn't the only source of iron. Many vegetarian foods contain lots of it, including beans (like black beans and lentils), greens, and other vegetables. It is true that the iron in meat (called heme iron) is more easily absorbed than the iron in plants (called nonheme iron). But you can help your body absorb more plant iron simply by eating something containing vitamin C along with your iron-rich foods—something that you may already do without even trying. It's as easy as tossing back a little OJ or gobbling a handful of strawberries with lunch or dinner.

Myth #3: Your Bones Won't Grow If You Don't Drink Milk or Eat Cheese

Milk and cheese do, indeed, contain lots of calcium per serving. Milk even *looks* like it's good for bones and teeth, because it's white, but calcium-rich foods come in other colors too. For instance, certain green foods, such as kale, okra, collard greens, and Chinese cabbage, are excellent sources of calcium. In countries where people eat lots of leafy greens and sea vegetables but no dairy products, they have strong, healthy bones.

Dairy calcium is not "better" than plant calcium. The truth is, experts say, it's perfectly acceptable to get the calcium you need from sources other than dairy. But—and this is important—you have to know what you're doing. "Vegans in this country who stop consuming dairy products may have a hard time getting calcium unless they make an effort," says Virginia Messina, R.D., a practicing nutritionist who has written extensively about vegetarian issues. First, you have to learn about what plant foods are good calcium sources. (See the list in chapter 10.) Second, you have to eat plenty of calcium-rich plant foods on a regular basis (like, every day). Third, experts say that it's a real challenge for you to get all of the calcium you need (teens need a lot) just from these foods; they say you should also include foods that have been *fortified* with calcium, such as calcium-fortified orange juice and soymilk. Tofu made with calcium salts (such as calcium sulfate) is another really good source of the mineral. If you're not prepared to eat lots of calcium-rich foods—and it's *not* always practical to do so in today's fast-food world—nutrition experts advise you to take a supplement. Bottom line: You have to get your calcium from *somewhere.*

Here's something else to remember: The calcium in your diet is just one part of the strong-bone story. Also important to keep in mind are: (1) Exercise. Bones are alive and respond to use, just like muscles do. When you use them, they become stronger. (2) Vitamin D. You get it by spending time in the sun. (Milk is fortified with it.) (3) Calcium loss. A diet heavy in animal protein is known to cause calcium loss in adults (sugar, salt, and caffeine are suspect, too), although it's not clear exactly what happens in teens. "What we're really talking about is building a healthy skeleton," says Michael Klaper, M.D., director of the Institute of Nutrition Education and Research and author of *Pregnancy, Children and the Vegan Diet* (Umatilla, FL: Gentle World, 1987). "That requires that you think about these other things besides just how many grams of calcium you get."

Myth #4:   Vitamin B_{12} Deficiency Is Common Among Vegans

B_{12} deficiency among vegans is rare, even though there is no plant source of the vitamin. And although animal products such as meat, eggs, and milk contain B_{12}, most B_{12} deficiencies occur among people who eat those products, which makes doctors think that a B_{12} deficiency might have to do with other things going on in the body as well. Even though your body needs only small amounts of it, vitamin B_{12} is very important for proper nervous-system function, so you should make sure to get it in your diet. If you don't eat dairy products, you can eat foods fortified with B_{12}, such as many breakfast cereals, pastas, crackers, and other prepared foods. If you're not into reading labels to see what products contain B_{12}, you should take a supplement.

WHAT YOU CAN DO

● Read up on vegetarian health and nutrition. Contact the American Dietetic Association for its pamphlet "Eating Well—The Vegetarian Way." Write the ADA at 216 West Jackson Boulevard, Chicago, IL 60606-6995.

- If you (or your parents) are not convinced of the health benefits of a vegetarian diet, check out other resources on vegetarian health. For instance, *Vegetarian Times* magazine publishes current news about veggie health and nutrition every month.

- Write a term paper about a vegetarian-related health topic. Tauna Houghton, 18, of Bainbridge Island, Washington, wrote about the down side of dairy products for her senior class project. Specifically, she investigated how much of the public's nutrition information comes from the dairy industry itself. Her audience was intrigued, she says: "One of the teachers had me present it to two of his classes."

BUT WHAT ABOUT CHICKEN AND FISH?

Chicken and fish are better for you than red meat, right? Well, not so fast:

- *A three-ounce serving of chicken or turkey contains the same amount of cholesterol as a similar-sized steak.*

- *Single servings of chicken and turkey do contain less saturated fat than red meat, but few people eat a single serving. At many restaurants, a serving size equals half a chicken—which has perhaps been dipped in batter and fried.*

- *Some types of fish receive more than half of their calories from fat.*

- *Both poultry and fish have safety problems. According to a report in the* Los Angeles Times, *the United States Department of Agriculture knows that as much as 60 percent of raw poul-*

try is contaminated with the disease-causing salmonella bacteria. (Proper cooking kills harmful food bacteria, but some people prefer to avoid meat altogether.) A Consumer Reports *investigation found that fish don't fare much better. Nearly one-half of the fish it tested was contaminated by bacteria from human or animal feces, and some fish were contaminated with PCBs (a potentially cancer-causing agent) and mercury (which may harm the nervous system).*

ONE BURGER . . . HOLD THE BACTERIA

What hidden nasties lurk in that burger or turkey sandwich?

BACTERIA: *Things like salmonella and* E. coli. *When a 1993* E. coli *outbreak from contaminated hamburger caused death and many illnesses, even the government admitted that its meat-inspection system isn't up to snuff.*

ANTIBIOTICS: *Veterinary drugs are used to treat sick animals and to make them grow faster, but are they safe for humans who eat those animals? According to the Center for Science in the Public Interest, a 1985 government report said that as many as 90 percent of the drugs used had not yet been approved by the U.S. Food and Drug Administration as safe and effective for animals or humans.*

HORMONES: *Two out of every three beef cattle are implanted with hormones to produce leaner, cheaper meat. It's common for new hormones—like those developed for dairy cows—to be used in the food supply even before it is known whether they're completely safe for humans.*

CHEMICAL PESTICIDES: *Although we think of pesticide residues as occurring mostly in fruits and vegetables, a 1988 Canadian study found some of the highest pesticide residues in meat and eggs.*

PART 2

~~~

HOW TO MANEUVER IN A MEAT-EATING WORLD

CHAPTER 5

MAKING THE SWITCH

"The guy who invented headcheese must have really been hungry."

—*Jerry Seinfeld*

So you've decided to give this vegetarian thing a try. But how should you do it? Do you simply stop eating all meat overnight? Or should you ease into it? Where do you draw the line? And what if you mess up? Don't worry; all vegetarians have questions when they're first getting started.

HOW SHOULD YOU DO IT?

You can go vegetarian all at once, or very slowly. Neither way is "right" or "wrong." And either way can be perfectly healthy.

The Overnight Vegetarian

Some people are able to make big changes in their diets in what seems like the blink of an eye. "Well, I just did it," says 17-year-old Lynnise Phillips. "I stopped eating meat all in one day. It was pretty random. My mom had steak for dinner and I was like, 'Ew, I don't want to eat this anymore.'" Some people even decide to cut out all animal products at once: meat, eggs, even milk. That's what Mike Ruiz did. "I just dropped every-thing. Cold turkey." (No pun intended.) It wasn't always easy for him, but since he felt so strongly about not eating animal products, he wanted to try diving right in.

The advantages of this approach? Some people find that it's actually *easier* to break away from meat if you just stop eating it, period. If you eat a little meat here and there, they say, you continue to tease your taste buds, and it just makes the whole transition more difficult. People also say that it feels satisfying to commit to something and stick to it.

But this all-or-nothing approach can have its drawbacks, too. If you have no idea what to eat, you might end up surviv-ing on french fries and soda, which isn't such a healthy diet. And some people simply don't feel comfortable changing so suddenly. "I tried to cut everything out all at once, and I just felt like, this is so drastic," says 16-year-old Rachel Seed. "When you're so used to eating meat, you might just break down and eat it again if you change that fast." No big deal. Try again, taking it more slowly.

The Gradual Vegetarian

You can also take your own sweet time switching to a vegetar-ian diet—over several months, several weeks, or even over years. "It's a process," says Darryl Neate, 17. You can go at it any number of ways. Suggests Rachel: "I think it should be done like one animal at a time." You might cut out red meat one month, then chicken, then fish. Or cut back on the number of meals each week that contain meat. You can also rearrange your meals so that meat is no longer the entrée. Use it as a small side dish or for flavoring instead. Eventually, if it feels right, drop it altogether.

The advantage of the gradual approach? It's simply less abrupt. You'll be making a positive change in your life without feeling overwhelmed. Plus, your parents might be more willing to support your choice to be vegetarian if you don't do it all at once. Some teens feel like they get stuck, though, if they take things too slowly. For one thing, it's easy to fall into the substitution trap: You cut out red meat, but load up on chicken. Or you cut out meat, but load up on dairy products. "I ate a *lot* of cheese when I started," says Julie Gerk. An alternative? Eat *some* cheese, if you'd like, but experiment with other foods, too, like new grains and veggies.

Whatever approach you decide to take, remember to give yourself some room to play around. Pay attention to what feels comfortable to you. "Whatever you do, and however long it takes to get rid of meat in your diet, is fine," says Esther Brienes, 19. "Even if you cut out one hamburger a week, you're doing something, and you're making a difference. Don't lose hope."

And don't be too hard on yourself (like, "If I don't give up eggs by next Thursday, I'm a failure."). Setting goals is fine, but forget about following the perfect schedule. Trust yourself to let your diet evolve. Eventually you'll find yourself exactly where you want to be.

WHERE DO YOU DRAW THE LINE?

The questions may be racing through your head: Is it enough just to stop eating red meat? Does my ultimate goal have to be giving up *all* animal products? If it's not, should I even bother doing anything? What if I really don't want to stop eating cheese pizza? What if I'm not ready to give up fish right now? What if I never will be? What if, after being vegetarian all year long, I decide to eat turkey on Thanksgiving? Am I a failure? What if I accidentally eat meat? And what about leather? Do I have to give away all of my leather shoes? Will people think I'm radical and weird if I do?

Yikes! That's a lot to think about. It's common to wonder whether you're doing "enough." It's easy to get discouraged. Donna Hope, 16, of New York state, has been working on becoming a vegetarian for two years now and is making slow and steady progress. "But when I found out that a total vegetarian doesn't even eat *dairy* products, I said, 'Wow, I don't know if I can do *that.*'"

Relax. Take things at your own pace, and as far as *you* want to take them. If you want to stop eating red meat, and that's all, then just stop eating red meat. Maybe you'll eventually stop eating other meat, too, but don't get caught up in a guilt trip if you don't. Celebrate that you have successfully given up red meat. That's something!

If you'd like to be a stricter vegetarian, but are struggling with it, be patient. You've already taken steps toward your goal. That's how Laurel Wilson, 15, sees it: She'd rather not eat dairy products, but it's hard for her to find foods that don't contain milk. But she's okay with that. "I'm happy with where

I'm at. I'm doing as much as I can right now. As long as I'm not eating meat, I figure I'm doing some good."

If you decide to eat meat on special occasions, so be it. Maybe you'll feel the need to eat turkey on Thanksgiving. Or, even though you swore off dairy products, you'll eat the cake made with milk and eggs that your grandmother made for your birthday. Perhaps you aren't ready to give up old family traditions, or perhaps you think it's more important not to hurt your grandmother's feelings than to take a stand against the dairy industry. Says Jeremy Blackman: "Occasionally I'll eat meat as a concession to someone who made it, or when I feel it's appropriate. I will turn it down, though, if I can without offending the person." Some people might challenge your commitment if they see you eating meat. ("Hey, I thought you were a vegetarian!") But what you eat and when you eat it is *your* business.

WHAT IF YOU MESS UP?

Every so often, you might eat something that you wish you hadn't. Maybe, in a moment of weakness, you break down and eat a slice of pepperoni pizza. Or you get to the bottom of your soup, which the waiter swore was vegetarian, only to find a chunk of chicken staring you in the face. What now? Has all of your effort simply gone down the drain?

There's no reason to feel guilty about an occasional slip-up. And if you make an exception to your diet, it doesn't mean you've failed. Julie Gerk usually doesn't eat eggs, "but if I'm at a restaurant and we're ordering something to share and everybody orders something with egg in it, then I might say, 'Well,

I'm going to eat egg today. But just because I eat an egg today doesn't mean that I'm going to eat it tomorrow. I'm still eating with this awareness.'" It's helpful to look at your vegetarian diet as a process, something that's always growing and becoming and evolving. On the other hand, you're always free to scrap the whole thing if it doesn't feel right. At least you will have tried.

Some teens are able to stick to their commitment to vegetarianism without wavering. And that's great. But this is an imperfect, meat-eating world we live in. No matter how strict and well-meaning you are, you might accidentally eat something containing meat broth or something else that upsets you. If that happens, brush it off. Just focus on all of the positive things you've achieved by changing your diet: You've saved some animals, you've helped lessen the burden on the environment, and you've improved your own health. Do what you can, and feel good about it. When it comes to being a vegetarian, there are no mess-ups. Only experiences.

WHAT YOU CAN DO

- Read, read, read all about it. Browse through vegetarian magazines and cookbooks to learn all you can about meatless living.
- Approach a vegetarian diet in a way that's comfortable for you. "I started out with familiar foods first," says David. "At first I ate a lot of soups, like vegetable and minestrone, and a lot of pasta and pizza and peanut butter and jelly. *Then* I threw in some new foods."
- Surround yourself with support! It's more fun to make a change when you're not doing it alone. "It's easier when

you have a network—people to share recipes and ideas with," says Jennifer Neate, 19, of Ontario, Canada. Check around your school for other vegetarians, or ask the clerk at your local natural food store if there is a vegetarian society in your town. Or contact one of the groups listed in Appendix 1.

● Become a vegetarian pen pal. Share ideas and encouragement with other young vegetarians. You can find a pen pal through the Vegetarian Resource Group, the North American Vegetarian Society, or People for the Ethical Treatment of Animals. (See Appendix 1.)

HOW EASY *IS* IT TO GO VEGGIE?

"Man, I don't know how you do it." That's what 16-year-old Eliza Hollingshead's friends say to her when they find out she's a veg. A lot of people think being a vegetarian sounds hard. Is it? Or is it easy? That just depends on whom you ask. Here's what some teens say:

"Generally, I'd say it's easy. When something comes out on the national news saying people just died after eating at a fast-food restaurant, then it's easy. When I read how fat and cholesterol cause heart disease, then it's easy. When I read about cancer and its connection to a high-fat diet, then it's easy. But for someone who's not strong-willed, it could be tough. But I don't mind being a nonconformist."

—John, 17

"It was really easy for me to give up meat, so that's why it's hard for me to understand why

other kids might say, 'I just like the taste of meat too much.'"   —Tina, 18

"It was really hard for me not to eat chicken, because my family is like Chicken Family of America."   —Heather, 18

"A lot of people are afraid of making the transition, or being different. One guy I know was really embarrassed about it. He thinks he'll be thought of as a wimp if he cares about animals."   —Holly, 19

"It's really hard. I've been a vegetarian for about five months: no meat, no chicken, no fish, no dairy, no eggs. I really like meat. I really miss it. But I doubt I'll go back."   —Mike, 17

LEATHER: A TOUGH QUESTION

It happens to every vegetarian sooner or later: A skeptical person walks up to you, looks down at your feet, and asks: "If you're a vegetarian, how come you wear leather shoes?" What do you say? Should you jump right out of your loafers? Should you give your Air Jordans away to charity? Kristina Johnson, 18, has a joking way of answering back: "When someone asks, 'How can you wear leather shoes?' you can say, 'Well, those came off the hamburger you just ate.'"

Seriously, though, leather is a tough issue to deal with. The leather industry gets its supply of cowhide from the slaughterhouses, so when you buy leather shoes, you're supporting that business. Some teens avoid leather because they know that the process of tanning and dying leather pollutes the environment. Some people drop leather just as quickly as they drop meat. They see no difference between using an animal's meat and using its hide. As Anne Quistorff sees it: "They had to kill the animal to get the leather. They had to kill the animal to get the meat. I feel like they are equally important." Esther Brienes agrees: "If we have the capacity of clothing ourselves and feeding ourselves without taking another life, then we should do that."

But the issue gets a little complicated. "I will not buy leather," says John Lanzerotta, a vegan. "But I still have a pair of leather shoes that I had from two years ago, and I'll wear them until they fall apart." What kind of nonleather shoes can he buy when his leather ones give out? There are plenty of shoes out there made of man-made materials; even some big-name shoemakers have nonleather options. Unfortunately, many of these shoes are made from plastic, which poses environmental problems of its own. And because plastic shoes don't "breathe" like leather ones do, your feet will probably sweat more in them. Nor are they as durable as leather; you have to replace them more often. No pair of shoes is ethically perfect; even the cotton used to make your canvas hightops was probably grown *with a hefty dose of pesticides. It's up to you to weigh the pros and cons of the different products and choose the shoe that fits your beliefs.*

With some effort, you can find an animal-free alternative to nearly any leather item you currently use. But don't let someone else tell you what your personal ethics should be. Says Michelle, an 18-year-old vegan: "People will look at my belt and shoes and say, 'How can you wear that?' I just tell them that I'm taking it as far as I can."

Ready for a little sole searching? The Vegetarian Education Network can help you find nonleather shoes. Write to VE-Net at P.O. Box 3347, West Chester, PA 19381.

VEGETARIANS
ONLINE

Hey, computer heads, listen up. If you have access to a modem, you can connect with vegetarians from all over through one of the online services created especially for vegetarians. Such services are available through CompuServe, Prodigy, and Internet. Even if you can't hook up with others, you can still use your computer to learn about a vegetarian diet. For IBM compatibles, there's the Vegetarian Game, a program from the Vegetarian Resource Group. Test your knowledge of food, health and nutrition, famous vegetarians, and environmental and ethical issues. It's challenging for both beginner and expert veggies. Contact VRG, P.O. Box 1463, Bal-

timore, MD 21203. (Specify 3.5-inch or 5.25-inch disk.) For Macintosh, there's VegiCard, for the HyperCard program (version 2.1 and up) to teach you about a vegan diet. Contact Earth-Save, 706 Frederick St., Santa Cruz, CA 95062.

CHAPTER 6

WHAT WILL YOUR PARENTS SAY?

" I come from a family where gravy is considered a beverage."
—Erma Bombeck

Parents are funny. They say they want to know what you're up to, but when you tell them, they don't always like it. Don't be surprised if your parents aren't exactly thrilled when you tell them that you've decided to be a vegetarian. Many parents respond something like this:

"Not while you're living under *my* roof."

"Where did you get an idea like that?!"

"*What*, exactly, do you plan to *eat*?"

"You'll never get enough protein [or calcium, or iron, or whatever]."

Or you might even get the old guilt treatment: "What? Isn't my cooking good enough for you?"

From these reactions, you'd think you were telling them that you've decided to drop out of school or turn the basement into a shelter for stray rodents. Of course, not all parents react this way. Many parents are becoming vegetarians themselves and would like nothing more than for the whole family to join them. Fifteen-year-old Laurel Wilson says it was her mom's idea to go vegetarian; one day the two of them rummaged through the kitchen cabinets together and got rid of anything containing meat. But the more common story seems to go like this: "I really want to be a vegetarian . . . but my parents won't let me."

Want a tip? Things will go much more smoothly if you stop for a minute and think about things from their perspective.

WHERE THEY'RE COMING FROM

Most likely, your parents will be worried about nutrition. They really do care whether you get enough protein, iron, and so on. And for whatever reason, they might have it in their heads that a vegetarian diet can't possibly meet all of your body's nutritional needs. Of course, it's your job to tell them that they're *wrong*, but the trick is doing so in a nice, nonrebellious way.

They might think that a vegetarian diet is just plain weird. Some people still have a stereotype of vegetarians as eccentric hippies who live in communes, munching on bean sprouts and chanting. They'll probably feel much better when they learn that all sorts of people become vegetarians for all sorts of reasons (and that you have no immediate plans of running off to join a commune).

Your parents might think you're just going through a phase. "They thought I was just doing it to be trendy," says Carrie Wittman, 16.

They might think that a vegetarian diet will mean more work for them. Lynnise remembers exactly what her mom said when she became vegetarian four years ago: "She was like, 'I'm not cooking two different meals for everyone.'"

They will probably take your vegetarian diet personally. You know, like it's a sign that you're somehow rejecting everything they've ever done for you. Don't be surprised if this happens. Food is a pretty emotional issue. Jennifer, 19, says her parents felt like she was challenging their judgment when she went vegetarian. "They made it sound like my becoming a vegetarian was a confrontation to their authority." Her father, especially, was not pleased with her choice. "He took it very personally. He thought I was saying, 'No, I don't accept your values. I don't want to do things the way that you taught me.'"

These are issues that go beyond the plate, straight to the heart of what parenthood is all about. If your parents seem really sensitive about stuff like this, it doesn't mean you can't be a vegetarian. It just means that you should try to think about their feelings when you break the news. Jennifer, for instance, made sure to point out the positive side to her father. "I said, 'Look, I believe in a lot of other values that you taught me.'" Remember: *How* you tell your parents is very important. Which leads us to ...

HOW TO SOFTEN THE BLOW

There's no one right way to tell your parents that you've decided to become a vegetarian and no way to ensure that they're not going to freak out. But you can increase the chances that they'll hear you out.

Pick a Good Time to Tell Them

Right as your father is taking the carving knife to the Thanksgiving turkey and Aunt Bess is announcing her recipe for giblet gravy is not a good time. Too much family tradition is hanging in the air. In fact, any mealtime is probably not the best setting for breaking the news. A neutral, nonfood time might be better. Try to catch your parents when they're not preoccupied with something else. Let them know in a calm, confident voice that there's something you want to discuss with them. Don't sound too serious, though, or they'll probably be expecting some *really* bad news.

Keep a Cool Attitude

If you sound like you expect a confrontation, you'll probably get one. Explain your decision rationally. Run through your reasons with your parents. As one teen puts it, "They might not understand and they might be horrified, but if you discuss it rationally, they'll understand that you're serious about it." Let them know that you've given this a lot of thought.

Sound Well-Informed

Let your folks know that you've done your homework. Your best defense will be your ability to answer their questions. And they *will* ask questions. Show them books, magazines, and newspaper articles explaining what a vegetarian diet is all about. Substantiate your choice to go vegetarian with facts: If the environment is what matters to you, tell them why a meatless diet is better for the planet. If you're doing it for your health, show them what the health experts say. Careful: Don't get preachy! That I'm-right-you're-wrong attitude can be a real pain.

Calm Their Fears

If they swear you'll die of starvation, show them information from health experts saying that a vegetarian diet can be a perfectly healthy way to eat. (You can receive a pamphlet on vegetarian nutrition from the American Dietetic Association by writing to the ADA at 216 West Jackson Boulevard, Chicago, IL 60606-6995, or by calling (800) 366-1655.)

If it will make them feel better, tell them you'll go to see a doctor or registered dietitian. If you can arrange for a doubting parent to hear straight from a health expert that a vegetarian diet is healthy, you've got it made. Call the ADA hotline listed above to find a registered dietitian specializing in vegetarian nutrition.

Offer to Help with Shopping and Cooking

Your parents are more likely to approve of your new diet if they realize that it won't mean more work for them. They'll probably be very happy about this display of self-reliance— unless, of course, they find out that your idea of a nutritious dinner is french fries and ice cream. If you're really committed to this, you're going to have to learn how to cook a few things that are good for you. Don't worry! Lots of nutritious things are really easy to make.

Be Patient

It would be unfair of you to expect your family to understand your decision and feel comfortable with it overnight. Without fail, somebody in the family is going to get frustrated when you refuse to set foot in a restaurant because it fries its food in lard, and your mother will roll her eyes (at least!) when your first veggie lasagna drips all over the inside of her clean oven. Remember that your transition to a meatless diet is affecting everyone in the household, not just you. So whenever you get even the slightest sign of support, let your parents and siblings know that you appreciate it.

WHAT SHOULD YOU DO IF THE GOING GETS ROUGH?

If you're lucky, your parents will eventually come around and accept your decision. Most do. Once they realize that you're serious about making the change, and once they're convinced that you're not going to keel over and die anytime soon, their protests will probably become fewer and farther between. "When I first decided to be a vegetarian, I heard about it from my parents every day," says one teen. "Then there was just a *weekly* talk about it. Now they don't say anything."

Of course, things don't *always* go so smoothly. "My parents are still mad at me," notes Josh, a Seattle-area teen. Just when you thought you had your parents' support, they might throw a few stumbling blocks your way. Such as:

"Mom? Dad? What's This Meat Doing in My Chili?"

They wouldn't, would they? Actually sneak it onto your dinner plate? It's happened to 16-year-old Tennille Teague. "We'll be eating a casserole and I'll ask if there's cream of chicken soup in it, and they'll deny it. Then I'll find the cream of chicken soup can. When I show them, they'll say, 'Oh, I forgot,' or 'Oh, I thought it was cream of *mushroom.*' "

What should you do in a situation like that? Well, maybe your family wasn't really trying to trick you. Maybe they thought that, even though you don't eat meat, you don't mind eating things with meat broth or even meat that's well hidden. This would be a good time to explain to them exactly what a vegetarian diet is. Make sure you're clear on what you will and will not eat. If it turns out that they *were* trying to trick you, find out why. Are they still afraid that you can't survive without meat? Sit down with them again (sigh!), and go over the stuff on health and nutrition. (Check chapters 4 and 10.)

What If There's Nothing in the House for a Vegetarian to Eat?

Many vegetarians are able to get by on the same groceries as the rest of the family. But what if all your parents buy is meat-laden TV dinners? Or junk food? "My family thinks they can just buy macaroni and cheese and I'll be happy," says Tennille. "And they always want to buy iceberg lettuce. I want romaine, because it's more nutritious, but they say that I'm the only one who will eat it, and that it will go bad." If there's something that you'd like to add to the grocery list, explain what and why. Do you want to try tofu? Your parents, like most meat eaters, might think that tofu looks like nothing more than chalk-flavored

Jell-O. You'll have a better shot at landing some in the house if you explain: 1) That it's a good source of protein and other nutrients (they'll probably be impressed that you actually know about nutrition); and 2)That you have actual tofu recipes that you plan on making. Perhaps your folks are worried that strange new foods will go to waste. Assure them otherwise.

What If Your Parents Blame Every Little Thing on Your Vegetarian Diet?

It will happen the minute you catch your first cold as a vegetarian. "Aha! I knew it!" your father will exclaim. "It's that diet of yours!" Skeptical parents love to link every sniffle and scraped elbow to your meatless diet. They'll think your immune system is down because you no longer eat meat. One teen says her mother—no lie—thought her shinsplints had something to do with her diet. "She tried to associate every problem I had with my vegetarianism," says Carolyn Lewis. "She's not as concerned now. Now she only thinks I'm ridiculous. But that's okay. She can think I'm ridiculous."

What such parental reactions mean, of course, is that although they're trying their darnedest to hold their tongues, they're really still quite doubtful about vegetarianism. Try to enlighten them by playing up the positive. While they're busy listing all of the illnesses you'll get if you don't eat meat, you might rattle off all the things that you probably *won't* get, like heart disease and some cancers. If you're convincing, soon they might ask to try a little of that tofu that they didn't want to buy.

What If Your Parents Draw the Line?

If you thought your parents put up a fight when you told them you no longer eat meat, wait to see what happens if you decide to give up dairy, too. This is where most parents really put their foot down. "When I decided to go vegan, my parents thought I was totally radical," says 18-year-old Chy Lin. "They said, '*No way* are we letting you do that.'" (Of course, she did anyway.) Your parents are afraid that you won't get enough calcium for your growing bones. Let them know that you plan to get your calcium from other sources, like green vegetables and calcium-fortified foods. You might work out an agreement with them: Tell them that you'll take a calcium supplement until you're sure you know what you're doing.

What If Your Parents Simply Say No?

"My parents won't let me be vegetarian," says Phil, 17. He compromises by leading a sort of double life: He's not a vegetarian at home. "But outside of the house, I don't *touch* meat."

STICK WITH IT

Even if your parents come around, it's likely that you'll be up against other challenges from your family. "My brother will eat meat in front of me and be like 'Mmm, this dead cow is good,'" says Emily, 18. Some teens find that it takes extra sensitivity to explain their vegetarianism to their grandparents. "I understand that when my grandmother was young, there probably weren't many vegetarians at all," says Michelle. "I don't want to sound like I disrespect her beliefs, or tell her that she's wrong."

On the other hand, you might be pleasantly surprised at what happens in your household when you stop eating meat.

Even if your family is skeptical about vegetarianism now, you may be the reason they become vegetarian, too. Jennifer Neate says her family has begun to follow her example. "They've reduced the amount of meat they eat significantly. Before, at least once a week, they'd have roast beef or pork. Now that's very rare. Even though they don't agree with what I've been saying, they must be thinking that I make a little bit of sense." Sixteen-year-old Dennis says his family has come around. "At first my family didn't want me to be a vegetarian. Now I've got them all eating less meat."

WHAT YOU CAN DO

- Share your food! At your family's next big gathering (birthday, reunion, etc.), prepare a vegetarian dish for the potluck table. "I went to a family party and brought a banana tofu cream pie," says Holly, 19. "I just set it down with the other food and said that it had no animal products in it. They loved it. That's a really good way to show that vegetarians eat good food." Helpful hint: Don't make anything too weird; save the Sea Vegetable Surprise for another occasion.

- Educate your family. Maybe your parents would like to help you be a vegetarian but honestly don't know how. The North American Vegetarian Society has a booklet called "The Care and Feeding of a Vegetarian" that is full of ideas they can use. Write NAVS, P.O. Box 72, Dolgeville, NY 13329.

- Offer to make a vegetarian meal for the whole family.

**YOUR FIRST
TURKEY-FREE
THANKSGIVING**

Thanksgiving without turkey? Why not? When you think about it, turkey is just one small part of the traditional meal anyway. It's the autumn bounty—squash, sweet potatoes, nuts, apples, pumpkins, and cranberries—that really fills up the table.

There are a few ways to have a vegetarian Thanksgiving. One option is simply to eat around the turkey. Most Thanksgiving cooks make so many great side dishes that a vegetarian can easily leave the table as stuffed as anyone else in the family. But to make the day really special, why not prepare a dish to add to the feast? It can be as simple as a vegetarian gravy to cover your vegetables, or maybe some sort of casserole. Sixteen-year-old Erica Hammer says that her grandmother made an eggplant dish for her, plus a special turkeyless stuffing. Hint: If you use poultry seasoning (which doesn't actually contain any poultry), your stuffing will taste just like everybody else's.

If you're really adventuresome, you can make a fake turkey roast. There's an absolutely fantastic recipe for one in a cookbook called The Now and Zen Epicure *by Miyoko Nishimoto. It's quite a project, and it calls for some unusual ingredients, but you'll be amazed by the results. (You can order this vegetarian cookbook and others from the Book Publishing*

Company, P.O. Box 99, Summertown, TN 38483;
(800) 695-2241.)

GOING
AGAINST
TRADITION

When John Lanzerotta told his father that he was going to be a vegetarian, the main objection he received wasn't about nutrition. It was about culture. "My father said to me, 'You're Italian! Italians eat meat!'" When your diet clashes with your family's culture, it adds a whole new dimension to the situation. Anna Balla, 19, a student at the Art Institute of Chicago, is originally from Hungary. Her mother, Maria, agrees with her that a vegetarian diet is healthy. What she doesn't like is that Anna now cooks vegetarian dishes from other cultures (like Asian stir-fries and noodle dishes) instead of Hungarian goulash and stuffed cabbage. Says Anna: "She thinks I am losing my Hungarianism because I don't eat traditional things." Says Maria: "I'm jealous."

Meat plays a big role in many families' traditions. "I would go to family reunions, and with a black family, everything has meat in it," says Lynnise Phillips. "You don't make spaghetti without meat sauce. Even spinach has meat flavoring." Lynnise felt bad about abandoning tradition, but another big concern was simply finding something to eat. Nowadays, her mother takes along veggie dogs and burgers, just for Lynnise.

What do you do if diet clashes with culture?

It might help to talk things out. Let your parents know that just because you're eating differently, you're not rejecting your heritage. (In fact, in some cases, you may be eating more like your ancestors did before their diet became Americanized.) And don't forget to point out all of the family traditions that you still do celebrate.

CHAPTER 7

WHAT WILL YOUR FRIENDS SAY?

*"At first, there was some teasing. I was the only vegetarian
around. Then one of my friends became vegetarian, and there were
two of us, and so on. And the closer people have gotten to me,
the more they understand what I am doing."*

—*Erin Martinez, 14*

~~~~~~~~~~ Okay. You've convinced your parents (sort
of) to let you give this veggie thing a try. What will your friends
think of your new diet? How should you even tell them?

MAKING YOUR STATEMENT

There's no right or wrong way to let people know about your
new diet. Some teens take the low-profile approach. "Sometimes

I just let people come to me," says Nik Trendowski, 16, of Detroit. "People see that I've got a vegetarian meal, and they'll ask me about it." In other words, if people ask, tell them. If they don't, don't.

But maybe you don't want to keep quiet about something so important to you. So speak your mind! Come right out and tell people that you've decided to go vegetarian! You might even be surprised at how interested people are. Says Nik: "Sometimes people will ask me for advice about how to do it themselves." Try not to sound too self-righteous, says Fernando, 15. He knows firsthand. "I used to get kind of preachy at lunch, saying things like, 'Hey, did you know that that's a dead animal you're eating?' Now that I look back, I was the most annoying person." One thing is certain: No matter how you tell people, you'll soon discover how many vegetarians there really are. "I just started going to a new school, and the girl who sits down next to me says she's a vegetarian," says Natasha, 15. "I said, 'No way! So am I!'"

WHAT WILL PEOPLE SAY?

"New vegetarians want to know, 'How will my friends treat me?' " says Chy Lin, an editor of the *How On Earth!* newsletter. By and large, they'll treat you just fine. Says Chy: "Most of my friends respect me for being vegetarian. Most of them want to know more about it." It's pretty hip to be a vegetarian today, so you'll get fewer weird looks and responses than you would have, say, five years ago. "People will say, 'Oh yeah, I'm a vegetarian too'—sometimes even if they're not," says Lynnise.

Of course, some people find anything other than their own way of doing things an easy target for jokes and criticism.

"It was really hard for my friends to accept," says Erin, 14. "They weren't horrible about teasing me, but it was annoying. People like to show you meat and dangle it in front of your face. I'm not that sensitive to that kind of thing, but it was really starting to drive me crazy." Usually the teasing is light-hearted. "My friends call me Celery Man or Nature Man," says John. "Or they'll try to bribe me, saying, 'If you do this for me, I'll eat my veggies for a week.' "

QUESTIONS, QUESTIONS, QUESTIONS

Both friends and strangers will have something to say when they find out you're a vegetarian. "Most people will simply be curious," says one teen. Here's a sample of the comments you'll hear.

> **"BUT WHAT DO YOU EAT?"** *As if the only edible thing on this planet had legs and a face at one time. People are so used to thinking of meat as a main dish, they forget that other foods exist. Introduce them to the wonderful world of grains, beans, fruits, and vegetables.*

> **"WHY?"** *It's hard for some people to understand why you'd swear off burgers and chicken wings. You could tell them all that stuff about the animals, the planet, and health. Or you could simply say: "With all of the really cool plant foods available, why not be a vegetarian?"*

> **"BUT YOU EAT CHICKEN AND FISH, DON'T YOU?"** *When was the last time you saw a chicken or a fish growing in a garden? It's funny how some people think that birds and fish are vegetables.*

"SO, YOU JUST EAT SALAD?" *Some people think all that vegetarians munch on is lettuce leaves and carrot sticks. But vegetarians can rattle off long lists of what they eat: Pastas, stews, tofu dogs, nachos, stir-fries, and veggie burgers, not to mention great ethnic foods such as Thai noodle dishes and Indian curried vegetables. "When my friends come over to dinner, they're surprised that my cupboards are always full of great things to eat," says Laurel, 15.*

"DON'T YOU MISS MEAT?" *True, some vegetarians find that their mouths still water when they smell Mom's stroganoff or fried chicken. But not others: "Now that I think about it," says David, "I think it's just disgusting to put a dead animal in my mouth." Miss it? Yuck. No way.*

"HOW DO YOU GET ENOUGH PROTEIN?" *Yes, even after you've explained it to your parents, you'll have to explain it again to your friends—and the school nurse, your track coach, and just about everyone else. Learn the scoop on page 118.*

And now, for the most common response you may hear:

"A VEGETARIAN? COOL!" *Times are changing. Says Fernando: "People used to react like, 'You're a vegetarian? Oh my God, you're going to die.' Now people say, 'Wow, that's really good. I'm trying to cut back, too.'"*

You've picked a great time to get into a vegetarian diet.

THE GREAT DEBATE

You'll run into some folks who actually want to *argue* about your diet. Some of the arguments will be lame, and some will be well thought-out and intelligent. How can you deal with negative reactions from people? Here's what some teens say:

- "When people don't understand what you're doing, or what vegetarianism is, the best thing you can do is to teach them. Before you become a vegetarian, you should learn about it—the animal-rights stuff, the environmental stuff—because people are going to ask you questions. You have to be able to explain to them what you're doing."

  —Dennis, 16

- "The most important thing you can do is to educate yourself. It takes some work, but it's worth it. I know some people who, if you ask them why they're a vegetarian, all they say is that 'meat is disgusting.' Those are the people who are going to get harassed. If you can develop a good argument, people will say, 'Uh-oh, she knows what she's talking about,' and will leave you alone."

  —Samantha, 15

- "People tend to react strangely to vegetarianism. You can ignore what they say. Blow it off. Or explain to them. I usually say that I love animals very much, and it's very hard for me to think about eating them. I'll do it in a way that's not stepping on their toes, though. They have the right to think what they want."   —Erin, 14

- "I don't care what people think. I turn it all back on them. If they say to me, 'Why are you a vegetarian?' I say,

'Why aren't you?' If they say, 'How can you not eat meat?' I say, 'How can you eat it?'" —Jude, 18

● "I'm not going to try to change people's minds, but I'm not going to eat meat." —Jesse, 15

● "I gain more confidence when I talk to other people about it. It makes me think again about how I feel. I usually come up with even more reasons for being a vegetarian, and newer ways of looking at things."

—Michelle, 18

You'll quickly get the knack of dealing with the doubters. "Over the years, my answers to the same old questions have become much more diverse and sophisticated," says Lysbeth Guillorn, 20, of Connecticut, who has been a vegetarian since age 10. Still, don't get down if you don't turn everyone on to your new way of eating. Says Esther, 19: "I meet people who understand why I'm a vegetarian, but who say, 'Listen, I love meat. I love hamburgers. I'm not ready to give that up.'" Food is a very personal issue.

WHAT YOU CAN DO

● Don't just tell your friends that being a vegetarian is fun—show them! Invite friends on a picnic and pack a basket full of really hip vegetarian (or vegan) food.

● Write it down! Here's a good way to express your feelings about a vegetarian diet: Enter the Annual Vegetarian Essay Contest, sponsored by the Vegetarian Resource Group. Write about any vegetarian topic you want (you don't even have to be a vegetarian to enter). Emily Lux, 18, of New Jersey recently won the contest for her first-person essay titled "Omnivore, Schwomnivore." She won a savings bond, but she says that wasn't the best part of the prize: "This verified that there are other people who see my reasons for becoming a vegetarian." For more information about the contest, see page 190.

CHAPTER 8

STICKY SITUATIONS

*❝This is an ongoing process, and I'm learning new things
about myself and my diet every day.❞*

—*Andrea Arnold, 16*

〰〰〰〰〰〰 One thing that you'll immediately notice
when you become a vegetarian is how much this world is set
up for meat eaters. Once you start looking at things from a
vegetarian's point of view, you may have to relearn a few
things.

Like ordering from a menu. Say you're at a restaurant with
your family. The vegetable soup sounds good. But is it vegetarian? Most restaurant soups are made with chicken or beef
stock. Hmm. You'll have to ask about that. And that pasta

primavera sounds tasty, too, but what if they season the pasta sauce with meat stock? Hmm. Meanwhile, your family is hiding behind their menus, acting as if they don't know you. How can you ask for exactly what you want without being a pain to be around? "This is a really big issue between my friends and me," says Kristina, 18. "If we go out to eat together, they'll roll their eyes when I ask for a half vegetarian pizza, or whether the soup is made with beef stock. I don't want to alienate my friends." After all, who wants to feel like an oddball?

Being a vegetarian requires at least *some* sense of adventure. Sometimes it might seem like a struggle. You want to stick to your beliefs, but you want to fit in, too. Eventually you'll develop your own style for handling awkward situations and sometimes even keep them from happening in the first place. There are no hard-and-fast rules for getting out of jams. But here are some ideas.

THE FAST-FOOD FRENZY

Some vegetarians can't stand the thought of stepping into most fast-food places, especially burger restaurants. "It's kind of fun to boycott places like that," says one. You could suggest an alternative to your friends, like a pizza place where you could order a veggie pizza while they get pepperoni. But even at the meatiest fast-food restaurants, you *can* find a few things to eat:

> **SALAD.** *Of course, salad isn't* all *that vegetarians eat, but in fast-food land, it's often better than other choices. Fast-food salad bars, like the ones at Wendy's, are usually pretty good because you can pile on your own veggies and toppings. Note: Prepackaged salads sometimes contain meat or eggs.*

POTATO PRODUCTS. *Baked potatoes—plain or with veggie toppings—are a good option. Sometimes you can top them with salad-bar fixings. French fries aren't very nutritious, but they're something to eat when everyone else is chowing down. All the major burger chains now fry in vegetable shortening instead of lard (although they may fry meat products in the same fat, so check it out if that concerns you).*

HOLD THE MEAT. *You can always do the old "Give me a burger, hold the burger" routine and end up with a bun and some toppings but no meat. Buns at some places may contain animal fat (it varies from store to store at Burger King and Wendy's), so you may want to ask. At Taco Bell, you can get a burrito or soft taco made with beans only (they'll hold the cheese, too, if you'd like). It's common to find lard in refried beans, but Taco Bell doesn't use it. Yeah!*

By the way, here's a promising sign: Some of the major fast-food chains have test-marketed vegetarian burgers in this country and abroad. If you want something vegetarian on the menu, contact the company's management and lobby for it. Who knows? If enough people ask for vegetarian options, maybe someday you'll be able to walk into any fast-food place and *really* have it your way.

PARTY TIME!

You're at a party and a friend notices that you're not eating the spicy chicken wings that everyone else is chowing down on. You mention that you're a vegetarian. The room goes quiet. All of a sudden, you're the talk of the party, which is kind of fun for a while. But pretty soon, you just want something to eat, not attention.

"When I go to parties, there's really not much for me to eat," says Natasha, 15. A sure way to survive is to bring along a vegetarian dish that people can try, like a dip. One good option: hummus, a dip made with chickpeas, sesame paste, and garlic—even meat eaters really go for it. Going to a barbecue? Take along your own veggie burgers to grill.

DINING OUT, VEGETARIAN-STYLE

More restaurants than ever—even some steak houses—are serving meatless meals. That's because people are requesting them. According to the National Restaurant Association, 20 percent of American adults look for vegetarian meals when they go out to eat. It's a good idea to call ahead to make sure a restaurant will have a vegetarian dish. But remember, not all dishes that *sound* vegetarian necessarily are. You can't always trust, for instance, that the veget*able* soup is veget*arian*, or that the spicy Chinese bean curd isn't flavored with pork. The best idea is to ask before you order. Remember these tips:

DON'T BE SHY. *Waiters are used to getting all kinds of questions, including ones about vegetarian food. Most will be happy to check with the kitchen to ask whether a dish is vegetarian. A few things to ask about: beef, chicken, or fish stock in soups and sauces; eggs in pasta.*

BE STRAIGHTFORWARD. *Sometimes the simplest way to order is to tell the waiter, "I'm a vegetarian," and then say specifically what you will and won't eat. Ask the waiter to recommend something.*

It might surprise you to learn how many waiters are vegetarians themselves!

ASK FOR A CUSTOMIZED DISH. *Even if there's nothing vegetarian on the menu, don't despair. Many restaurants can change a dish to make it vegetarian. Ask if they can make the chicken-vegetable stir-fry without chicken, for instance. In the end, you could be eating the tastiest dish on the table.*

BE ADVENTURESOME. *If your family is up for it, try a new restaurant where there's lots of veggie fare. The menus of many ethnic restaurants (Thai, Ethiopian, Indian) are loaded with meatless choices.*

VEGGIE ETIQUETTE (OR, HELP! I'M HAVING A DINNER DILEMMA!)

Your friend's parents invite you for dinner. They know you're a vegetarian. That is, you *thought* they knew, until you're seated at their dinner table staring at tonight's special: Chicken Parmesan. Or perhaps they went out of their way to make a special vegetarian dish, but it contains eggs, which you don't eat. What do you do? Can you gracefully refuse without offending your host?

The best answer to this problem is to avoid it in the first place. Whenever you accept a dinner invitation, mention that you're a vegetarian and politely describe what that means: no chicken, fish, dairy, or whatever. This isn't being pushy. Most hosts would rather find out that you're a vegetarian *before* you arrive for dinner than as they're putting the meat on the table. If it seems like your host has no idea what to make for you, suggest something. You might offer to bring along a dish (people love this). Just make it sound like you don't expect anyone to go out of the way for you.

But it's easy to forget to plan ahead. "About once every two years or so, I'm over at a friend's house and I've forgotten to tell them I'm vegetarian," says Korum Bischoff, 18. What do you do if you find yourself staring that chicken in the face? Try to be polite to your host. You can come right out and explain that you don't eat meat or whatever else. Korum finds that people are pretty understanding. "I've never had anyone get mad at me about it." Some vegetarians are comfortable eating around the meat, but others aren't. Some vegetarians would rather make exceptions to their diet and eat the meat than offend a well-intentioned host. But chances are, there will be plenty of meat-free side dishes on the table that will fill you up, anyway. In any event, you should thank your host graciously for having you over for dinner. You'll both be better prepared next time!

DON'T GET THE TRAVELING BLUES

Once you've mastered being a vegetarian in your hometown, what do you do when you hit the road? Again, the rule of thumb is to plan ahead.

Going to summer camp? Find out ahead of time exactly what kind of food will be available. You may have to pack a survival kit of veggie food from home along with your sleeping bag and toothbrush. Nineteen-year-old Saffron Corsé, of Lansing, Michigan, learned the hard way: "When my sister Jade and I went to camp, there wasn't anything vegetarian for us to eat, even though my mom had given the directors special instructions. We basically starved." If you can travel away from your area, check out summer camps that cater to veggie campers, such as Au Grand Bois in Quebec, Canada. Write to VE-Net for more information about veggie camps: P.O. Box 3347, West Chester, PA 19381.

Going on a foreign-exchange program? Again, plan ahead. The American Field Service, or AFS, an organization that matches students with host families abroad, suggests telling your host family about your diet well in advance, to give them time to prepare. In some cultures, it won't be appropriate for you, as a young person, to make special dinner demands. Some young vegetarians decide to bend their own rules rather than appear disrespectful to their foreign hosts. On the other hand, many cultures eat vegetarian foods on a regular basis. And many vegetarians say a foreign-exchange experience is a great way to share their vegetarian cuisine—a growing part of American culture—with people in other countries.

WOULD YOU DATE A MEAT EATER?

He's really cute, but his breath smells like pepperoni. You're enthralled by her, but she's repulsed by your tofu sandwiches. Will this vegetarian thing ruin your love life forever?

As a vegetarian, you might find that it matters whether the person you date eats meat or not. Of course you'd like to think that the person of your dreams has as much compassion and good taste as you do. And you'd also like to be able to agree on what restaurants to visit, or be able to share a pizza.

Dating is one area where each vegetarian develops a unique policy about what to look for and what to put up with. "It's not that big of an issue," says Korum, "unless she's eating a big hamburger. That's kind of gross. And I don't like to share silverware with someone who's cutting into a steak." Says John, 17: "I would much rather date a vegetarian. I have problems with someone eating dead animals in front of me, but then again, I'm used to that." But what do you do if your heart speaks louder than your head? Most people realize that a policy to date only vegetarians could seriously limit their possibilities. "One guy I see right now eats meat," says Erica, 16. "If we got more involved it might matter, but right now I'm not going to say anything about it. It might put a damper on the relationship."

The important thing is for you to have confidence in your own life choices. What others will find attractive in you is your own sense of style and commitment to what you think is right. And who knows? Maybe there's a vegetarian lurking inside that special someone. "I would definitely go out with someone who is a meat eater," jokes Tina, 18. "But that's because I have enough confidence in myself that I think I'd be able to convince him to become a vegetarian too!"

A QUICK PEP TALK

You might be thinking that being a vegetarian is starting to sound like a lot of work: dealing with friends' comments, ordering at restaurants, getting out of awkward moments. And we haven't even gotten to what to *eat* yet.

Don't get discouraged. The best part about being a vegetarian is that it's something that only you can decide to do and something that only you can decide *how* to do. Yes, there are certain things that you should know about nutrition and what foods are good for you; we'll get to that. But as for your vegetarian style, well, that's *your* call, and yours alone. There's no test to take; there are no teachers to please.

Sure, people will ask you lots of questions about your diet. Sometimes they might make you feel like the oddball in the crowd because of what you eat (or don't). But how you approach each challenge that arises from your choice to be a vegetarian is simply for you to decide. You are the expert on you.

WHAT YOU CAN DO

- Tell restaurants exactly what you want! Talk to the managers of your favorite restaurants and request more vegetarian fare. Also, let fast-food joints know that you and the 12 million other vegetarians in this country would visit their restaurants more often if there were an all-vegetarian entrée on their menus. For a list of fast-food company addresses and phone numbers, contact the folks at the North American Vegetarian Society (NAVS), Box 72, Dolgeville, NY 13329; they'll send you a pamphlet about their Fast Food Campaign (which also lists animal-free foods available at specific restaurants). You can also ask your favorite fast-food restaurants for nutrition booklets listing the ingredients in all of their products.

- Celebrate with other vegetarians at a huge, meat-free party. Every summer the NAVS holds its Vegetarian Summerfest. Veggies from around the country get together to share information, food, and fun. Contact NAVS for more info. Also, the Vegetarian Resource Group sponsors summer trips for anyone who wants to attend. Call (410) 366-VEGE.

HOW TO FIND VEGGIE FOOD ANYWHERE

Here's a trick for finding a vegetarian restaurant while traveling: Just look up "health food store" in the local Yellow Pages and call and ask someone at the store where you can get vegetarian food in town. (Natalie Merchant, lead singer for the now-defunct group 10,000 Maniacs, says she uses this trick while on the road. It's a technique she picked up from R.E.M. singer Michael Stipe.) For a more direct approach, check out the Vegetarian Journal's Guide to Natural Foods Restaurants in the U.S. and Canada *from the Vegetarian Resource Group. It lists more than 1,500 restaurants. Contact the VRG at P.O. Box 1463, Baltimore, MD 21203.*

FLY THE VEGGIE SKIES

Traveling by air anytime soon? When you make your reservations, don't forget to request a vegetarian meal or snack for your flight. You can specify how strictly vegetarian you want your meal to be (ovo-lacto or vegan, for instance). Airlines will happily accommodate you. If you forget to make special meal arrangements when you reserve your tickets, you can still call the airline up to the day before the flight and make your request.

CHAPTER 9

SURVIVING AT SCHOOL

"Everybody's a pacifist between wars. It's like being a vegetarian between meals."

—*Colman McCarthy,
columnist for* The Washington Post

~~~~~~~~~~~~~Some of your biggest challenges as a new vegetarian may occur where you spend a whole lot of your time: at school. Here are some ideas to help you out.

THE SCHOOL LUNCH SITUATION

The Putney School, a small private school in Putney, Vermont, is a vegetarian student's paradise. Every day a vegetarian option is served, and sometimes it's the only dish available. Students at Putney also grow their own organic vegetables and even learn to make tofu!

But let's face it. Most school cafeterias are a far cry from Putney's. Your school probably serves burgers. Meat tacos. Spaghetti and meatballs. Sausage pizza. It's puzzling, considering that government health experts keep telling us to eat a low-fat, high-fiber diet. But the school lunches that our government funds are exactly the opposite: They are high in fat, low in fiber, and loaded with meat and cheese.

Why do these foods show up on your school's menu? Chances are, your school probably participates in the same national lunch program that most schools do. Through this program, schools get free meat, cheese, milk, and butter from Uncle Sam. Why doesn't the government give your school healthier ingredients? Although the U.S. Department of Agriculture (USDA) tells people to eat more fruits and vegetables, it also spends lots of money helping farmers produce more meat and dairy products than this country can reasonably use. The government then buys that surplus of animal products and donates it to schools. To make sure that schools serve you these ingredients, the government makes rules about what kinds of meals are allowed to be served. And if a school doesn't follow the rules, it won't continue to get government donations.

One of the rules that school cafeterias must follow is that each lunch must include a specific amount of meat or "meat alternate." That *sounds* like it leaves room for all types of vegetarian foods, but it doesn't. Some things, like beans and rice, are allowed. Others, like soybean burgers, are not (although soy is allowed to be mixed with meat). Makes sense, huh? The fact is, school lunches are more a matter of politics than common sense: The meat and dairy industries lobby our government to keep their products on your plates.

Fortunately, a growing number of food-service directors (the folks in charge of the cafeterias) are recognizing that young people are fed up with so much meat on their trays. Both parents and students are telling the schools that they want more vegetarian options and less high-fat, high-cholesterol food. Recently, a vegetarian lasagna was featured as a part of National School Lunch Week in schools around the country. At some schools, foods like vegetarian lasagna and meatless pizza make it onto the menu on a more regular basis. These foods are still high in fat and heavy on dairy (so vegans can't eat them), but they're a start.

HOW TO CHANGE *YOUR* CAFETERIA

Wouldn't it be great if you could enter the cafeteria line and find a vegetarian lunch waiting for you? That's a reality now at the junior high schools and high schools in Santa Cruz county, California, and some schools in Madison, Wisconsin, too. The change has come about through the efforts of a progressive program called the Healthy School Lunch Program, a project of the environmental organization EarthSave.

Here's the story: The Healthy School Lunch Program first talked with city and district school officials and then spent time educating teachers, principals, and students about the health benefits of a low-fat, plant-based diet. Then they worked with food-service directors to come up with nutritious, low-fat meals that feature fresh fruits and vegetables and whole grains. The entrées that are available—things like pizza, veggie burgers, burritos—are usually vegan. How did the students respond? In Santa Cruz schools, the vegetarian meals have been selling out every day.

The directors of the Healthy School Lunch Program want you to have the choices that students in Santa Cruz and Madison have. They are meeting with school-lunch policymakers in Washington, D.C., to encourage nationwide school-lunch reform. "We're trying to enlighten them," says Todd Winant, the project's codirector. "We're saying children deserve a choice."

You can create change in your own school. The folks at EarthSave have published *The Healthy School Lunch Action Guide*, a handbook that you can use to get started. In it, you'll learn exactly how to work for change in your own school district, plus where to write to encourage political leaders to improve school-lunch standards nationwide. (The book also includes curriculum ideas for teachers, recipes for food-service directors, and helpful information for parents.) Call (800) 362-3648 to order. Also, consider these tips, suggested by various vegetarian students around the country who have successfully changed their cafeteria menus.

> **BE ORGANIZED AND MATURE.** *Don't just complain about the food as you're passing through the cafeteria line. Arrange a meeting with your food-service director and a representative from the school administration, and tell them there is a need and demand for healthy, vegetarian food. Put together some information showing how healthy a vegetarian diet really is.*
>
> **BE SPECIFIC.** *Tell them exactly what you mean by the words* healthy *(e.g., not dripping with five pounds of cheese) and* vegetarian *(e.g., no ham flavoring in the beans and rice, and no fish).*

BE POLITE AND RESPECTFUL. *Let the food-service director and the cooks know that you understand that they have certain limitations to what they can do.*

BE A GOOD BUSINESS NEGOTIATOR. *Let them know that your school's vegetarian students want to continue eating in the cafeteria, but that it's difficult given the current menu. All cafeterias want to keep their customers.*

BE FRIENDLY AND HELPFUL. *Supply some vegetarian recipes and offer to get a group of students together to conduct a taste test, so the director knows that students will like the meatless meals before any menu changes are made. For recipe ideas, suggest:*

Vegetarian Quantity Recipes *from Vegetarian Resource Group, P.O. Box 1463, Baltimore, MD 21203. Available at a discount for students.*

Campus Favorites *from Dietitians in College and University Food Service. Contact ADA/DICUFS, c/o Susan Davis-Allen, M.S., R.D., 605 South Madison St., Lancaster, WI 53813.*

The Gold Plan Institutional Nutrition Program *from Physicians Committee for Responsible Medicine, 5100 Washington Ave., N.W., Suite 404, Washington, DC 20016.*

BE GRATEFUL AND SUPPORTIVE WHEN CHANGES *ARE* MADE. *If the cafeteria does get a vegetarian meal on the menu, round up friends to try it. If no one chooses the new meal after all, the director may decide to drop the whole thing. Tell*

your friends to call or write to the food-service direc-
tor (or just stop by during lunchtime) to say thank
you!

BE PATIENT. *Change isn't going to happen*
overnight. But at least you will have taken the first
step toward making your school more vegetarian-
friendly.

THE SCIENCE CLASS CLASH

The cafeteria isn't the only room at school where your vegetarian beliefs may be put to the test. What if your biology class requires you to dissect animals? Many vegetarian teens think it's
just as wrong to dissect animals as it is to eat them. Schools
usually purchase animals for dissection from biological supply companies that may get the animals or animal parts from
slaughterhouses, pet shops, or even animal control centers.
Recent investigations of biological supply companies have
uncovered brutal handling of animals that eventually end up
on the dissecting tray. But what can you do if you object to dissecting? Won't you flunk class if you don't participate?

Actually, there are several alternatives for learning about
anatomy, and you have every right to ask to use one of them.
"It's okay to say no to dissection," says Pat Graham, "and a
growing number of kids are." Pat is the mother of Jenifer
Graham, a student who sued her California high school when
it wouldn't permit her to use an alternative learning method.
Although Jenifer's case was settled out of court, her testimony
helped bring California students the right to object to dissection on moral grounds. Jenifer, an ethical vegetarian, even had

an after-school movie made about her story. And Pat has established a hotline for students who want to learn more about objecting to dissection: (800) 922-FROG.

How can you learn about anatomy if you don't dissect? There are a number of tools you could use, including computer programs that take you step-by-step through a dissection, or three-dimensional plastic models. By the way: If you live in California, Florida, or Pennsylvania, there are even laws saying that you have the right to use one of these alternative methods. Some other states and major cities also have policies, although not actual laws, saying that you have the right to object to dissection.

WHAT YOU CAN DO

- Start a vegetarian group in your school! Chances are, there are other people who would love to get together and share their veggie experiences and ideas. You could meet for a potluck at someone's house, or just get together after school to talk. It's nice to have a network of like-minded people to hang out with. For information on starting a vegetarian group, contact VE-Net, P.O. Box 3347, West Chester, PA 19381; (717) 529-8638, or the North American Vegetarian Society, P.O. Box 72, Dolgeville, NY 13329; (518) 568-7970.

- Teach others! One way to educate your classmates about vegetarian issues is to use vegetarian topics for term papers, book reports, speeches, or science fair projects. For science or ecology class, for instance, you might write a paper on how much water is used or how much soil is lost in meat production. In health class, you could discuss the benefits of a low-fat, vegetarian diet. Amber, 14, did a project about vegetarianism for her social studies class. "From doing the report, I learned that there were about ten people who are vegetarian in my class."

● Talk to your science teacher about alternatives to dissection. First, do your research and learn how to deal with arguments that will come up, as well as what alternatives are available. Call the Dissection Hotline at (800) 922-FROG. If you're in grades 7-12, director Pat Graham will send you a copy of *Objection to Dissection: A Student Handbook.* If you're younger, you'll get a book called *Saying No to Dissection.*

● Talk to your school administrators about including vegetarian issues in the school's curriculum. For more information, contact VE-Net, P.O. Box 3347, West Chester, PA 19831; (717) 529-8638.

● Deck your school's halls with veggie information. Holly Friel, 19, received permission from the school librarian to fill a display case with educational materials about vegetarianism. "It focused on three reasons why people become vegetarian—health, the environment, and animal rights," she says. (And the librarian appreciated not having to design the display, for once!)

VEGETARIANS MAKE THE YEARBOOK *At Eastwood High School in El Paso, Texas, the class of '93 wanted future generations to know that their school isn't home to just cowboys and cowgirls. That's why they added a page to their yearbook that would tell the story of their*

*school's vegetarians. "You may not realize it," be-
gins the article, "but there are more than 20 vegetarians in this school alone. Each of them has
individual reasons for vegetarian beliefs." The
article focused on students who have ethical
reasons for not eating animals. Lest anyone
have the idea that vegetarians only engage in
subversive, radical activities, the yearbook page
features a photo of one Eastwood vegetarian en-
gaged in some very normal behavior—prepar-
ing hall decorations for homecoming. "No
matter what their reasons for being vegetarian
are," the article ended, "these students said they
plan to stick to them for generations to come."*

PART 3

~~~~~~~~~~

BUT
WHAT
DO YOU
EAT?

CHAPTER 10

SOME NUTRITION BASICS

"It is nearly fifty years since I was assured by a conclave of doctors that if I did not eat meat I should die of starvation."

—George Bernard Shaw

It's time to get down to business. All of this information about telling your parents and handling sticky social situations won't mean a thing if you don't know what to eat in the first place. This brings us to a crash course in vegetarian nutrition.

Some of you probably couldn't care less about nutrition. But some of you do care; one concern heard over and over again from young vegetarians is: "What should I be eating in order to get what my body needs?" The following information is from nutrition experts such as registered dietitians, doctors, and others. (Don't yawn: It's actually pretty interesting. This is material that you can really *use*.)

THREE SIMPLE STEPS

Some people think it's really hard to put together healthy vegetarian meals. Actually, it's easy, although you can't just replace the meat in your diet with any old food—after all, if you eat french fries for lunch every day and macaroni and cheese for dinner every night, you will be a vegetarian, but not a very healthy one. But there are basically just three things you need to do to put together a healthy diet:

1. Learn a little nutrition trivia. What nutrients does your body need? Where can you get them?
2. Eat a variety of foods, to cover all the bases (and to make things more fun).
3. Watch out for a few common pitfalls, like eating too much junk food.

How much do you need to do to make your diet healthy? That depends. When many Americans drop the meat from their diet, they're not left with very much: some white bread, cheese, potatoes (in the form of fries or chips), and maybe some salad made from iceberg lettuce. That's not the most nutritious diet. But if you already eat a lot of vegetables, fruits, and grain products, you're well on your way.

NUTRITION NEWS YOU CAN USE

These are the things that your body needs for it to run right.

Carbohydrates

Carbohydrates, especially complex carbohydrates, provide the fuel that keeps your body going. One important type of complex carbohydrate is starch, which you'll find in grains, beans, and vegetables. If you play soccer or run on your school's track team, complex carbohydrates are the number-one fuel that you should choose to give you energy. But everyone, not just athletes, should eat more of these; in fact, they should make up most of your diet. One of the easiest ways to get them is to be a vegetarian, eating vegetables, grains and cereals, pasta (which is made from grain), dried beans and peas (also called legumes), seeds, and nuts. Meat and dairy products contain very little or no complex carbo-hydrates at all.

Fiber

Fiber sounds like something that only old people need to think about, but everyone—even a young person like you—could probably use a little more. Fiber is actually another kind of complex carbohydrate. There are two kinds of fiber (soluble and insoluble), but we'll skip the complicated chemistry defi-nitions and just leave it at this: When you have a diet with a good amount of fiber, you have less fat, lower cholesterol, lower risk of heart disease and colorectal cancer, and easier (ahem) elimination. And here's the important part: Only plants contain fiber. No animal products do. You can get it in veggies and grains, but legumes such as black beans and lentils are especially good sources. So are many breakfast cereals.

Protein

Protein is really important at any age, but especially at yours, because your body needs it to grow (and to do routine maintenance, too). How much do you need? The Recommended Dietary Allowances (RDAs) are:

> Girls: 11 to 14 years: 46 grams
>   15 to 18 years: 44 grams
>   19 to 24 years: 46 grams
> Boys: 11 to 14 years: 45 grams
>   15 to 18 years: 59 grams
>   19 to 24 years: 53 grams

If these numbers don't mean much to you, don't panic. Good nutrition is more than adding up grams of this and that. As long as you are getting enough calories and are eating a variety of foods, it's virtually impossible to be deficient in protein. You'd really have to go out of your way and eat a diet consisting only of low-protein foods like fruit and soda pop. You can get plenty of protein from legumes (like pinto beans and lentils), soyfoods (like tofu and tempeh), vegetables, nuts and seeds, as well as dairy products. If you eat things like pasta, vegetarian chili, bean burritos, stir-fries, peanut butter sandwiches or even potato salad, you're already getting lots of protein.

Fat

Your body needs some dietary fat—to process certain vitamins and for other things, too—so eating a totally fat-free diet is a really dangerous idea. But most people get too much fat, which can lead to health problems. How much is good? The general rule is that no more than 30 percent of your daily calories should come from fat, but more and more doctors are recommending that only 20 to 25 percent of your daily calories should come from fat, and some say even less, like 10 to 20 percent. Particularly bad for you is saturated fat, which is found mostly in animal products, as well as any type of fat that has been hydrogenated, such as the oil found in margarine and solid shortening. Dairy products can contain a lot of fat, so if you eat them, choose skim milk and low-fat cheese. Some plant foods are primarily fat, such as nuts and nut butters, avocados, and oils. That doesn't mean that you can't eat these foods; things like peanut butter sandwiches and guacamole dip add nutrients and variety to your diet. Remember, some dietary fat is good. Just don't make it the center of every meal. You can read more about calculating the amount of fat in your diet—and about *reducing* the amount of fat in your diet—in a book called *Simple, Lowfat & Vegetarian* by Suzanne Havala, M.S., R.D. (It's available from the Vegetarian Resource Group, P.O. Box 1463, Baltimore, MD 21203.)

Now for the vitamins and minerals.

Iron

Iron is important because it makes up hemoglobin, the part of the blood that carries oxygen through your body. A long-term shortage of iron could lead to iron-deficiency anemia. If you are a girl, you need more iron than boys do, because iron is lost every month when you menstruate. Girls age 11 to 24 need 15 milligrams a day; boys age 11 to 18 need 12 milligrams, but only 10 milligrams per day at age 19 and up.

Again, don't freak out too much about weighing and measuring grams of iron. It's easy to get all of the iron you need from a varied vegetarian diet. Many, many plant foods contain iron. (See the list below.) One reason vegetarians get enough iron is that their diets are usually high in vitamin C, which helps the body absorb plant iron. A very easy trick to getting the right amount of iron is to eat vitamin C–rich foods right along with iron-rich ones. It's so easy, in fact, that you're probably already doing it without thinking about it, like if you eat a burrito with beans (iron) and tomato or green pepper (vitamin C). Other ideas are bean chili with tomato sauce, or even a bowl of raisin bran (or other iron-fortified cereal) with a glass of orange juice. Another way of boosting your iron intake is to

IRON-RICH FOODS

Millet, ½ cup cooked: *7.0 mg.*

Lentils, 1 cup cooked: *6.6 mg.*

Blackstrap molasses, 2 Tbs.: *6.4 mg.*

Kidney beans, 1 cup cooked: *5.3 mg.*

Chickpeas, 1 cup cooked: *4.7 mg.*

Pinto beans, 1 cup cooked: *4.5 mg.*

Seitan, 4 ounces: *4.0 mg.*

Swiss chard, 1 cup cooked: *4.0 mg.*

Black beans, 1 cup cooked: *3.6 mg.*

Spinach, 1 cup cooked: *3.2 mg.*

Potato, baked, with skin: *2.8 mg.*

Sesame seeds, 2 Tbs.: *2.6 mg.*

Figs, 5 medium: *2.1 mg.*

Tempeh, ½ cup: *1.9 mg.*

Apricots, dried, 10 halves: *1.7 mg.*

Raisins, ½ cup: *1.6 mg.*

Tofu, 3 ½ ounces: *1.0 mg. to 9.6 mg.* (iron content of tofu varies among available listed sources)

cook in cast-iron pots or skillets. Some substances in coffee and tea can prevent your body from absorbing plant iron; herbal teas don't contain those substances.

Listed below are some vitamin C–rich foods (did you think you'd see *cauliflower* there?).

Calcium

You need calcium for strong bones. How much? The RDAs say that if you are a girl or boy between the ages of 11 and 19, you should get 1,200 mg. of calcium every day. There's some debate about this. On the one hand, some nutrition experts insist that the calcium recommendations for teens should be even higher. If you build up enough bone mass during your

VITAMIN C–RICH FOODS

Cranberry juice cocktail, 8 ounces: *108 mg.*

Orange juice, 8 ounces from frozen concentrate: *97 mg.*

Red pepper, ½ cup chopped: *95 mg.*

Papaya, ½ medium: *94 mg.*

Strawberries, 1 cup: *85 mg.*

Grapefruit juice, 8 ounces from frozen concentrate: *83 mg.*

Navel orange, 1 medium: *80 mg.*

Kiwifruit, 1 medium: *75 mg.*

Canteloupe, 1 cup pieces: *68 mg.*

Green pepper, ½ cup chopped: *64 mg.*

Kale, 1 cup cooked: *54 mg.*

Broccoli, ½ cup cooked: *49 mg.*

Brussels sprouts, 4 cooked: *48 mg.*

Cabbage, 1 cup raw: *34 mg.*

Cauliflower, ½ cup cooked: *34 mg.*

Raspberries, 1 cup: *31 mg.*

Tomato, 1 medium: *22 mg.*

Potato, baked, with skin: *26 mg.*

Sweet potato, baked: *28 mg.*

Parsley, 2 Tbs. chopped: *19 mg.*

Lemon juice, fresh, 2 Tbs.: *14 mg.*

teen years, the thinking goes, you may lower your risk of getting osteoporosis later. On the other hand, experts in vegetarian nutrition say that the RDAs, which were designed with meat eaters in mind, might not be appropriate for people who consume little or no animal protein (which has been linked to calcium loss from the body in adults). These experts point out that in other countries, the recommendations for calcium intake are much lower than they are here. Ironically, osteoporosis is much more common in the United States, even though people here get more calcium. The bottom line is that no one is totally sure exactly how much calcium you need, but health experts recommend playing it safe and getting *plenty.*

Where to get it? Everybody knows that dairy products contain calcium. As discussed in chapter 4, so do many plant foods, too. Kale, broccoli, bok choy, and turnip, mustard, and collard greens are especially good sources of calcium. So is tofu that is coagulated, or set, with calcium salts (such as calcium sulfate). Research shows that some calcium-containing plant foods, especially spinach, also contain substances that prevent your body from absorbing all the calcium. To make sure you're covering the bases, nutrition experts recommend including foods that have been fortified with calcium, too, like calcium-fortified orange juice and calcium-fortified soymilk. These foods are a real plus, especially if you think steamed kale sounds pukey.

Remember: Nutrition experts say that if you're not willing to make an extra effort to eat calcium-rich foods, you should take a supplement. That advice makes a lot of sense if you eat like most teens: french fries and PB & J sandwiches on the go.

CALCIUM-RICH FOODS

Collard greens, 1 cup cooked from frozen: *357 mg.*

Calcium-fortified orange juice, 8 ounces: *300 mg.*

Blackstrap molasses, 2 Tbs.: *274 mg.*

Firm tofu (processed with calcium sulfate)*, 4 ounces: *250 to 350 mg.*

Turnip greens, 1 cup cooked from frozen: *250 mg.*

Kale, 1 cup cooked from frozen: *180 mg.*

Broccoli, 1 cup cooked: *178 mg.*

Sesame seeds, 2 Tbs.: *176 mg.*

Calcium-fortified soymilk, 8 ounces: *160 to 300 mg.*

Chinese cabbage, 1 cup cooked: *158 mg.*

Figs, 5 medium: *135 mg.*

Navy beans, 1 cup cooked: *128 mg.*

Tahini (sesame butter), 2 Tbs.: *128 mg.*

Great northern beans, 1 cup cooked: *121 mg.*

Okra, 1 cup cooked: *100 mg.*

Tempeh, ½ cup: *77 mg.*

Arame (a sea vegetable), ¼ cup dry: *68 mg.*

*Tofu that's made with nigari, a mineral salt from seawater, contains less calcium.

Vitamin B$_{12}$

You just need a tiny bit of this vitamin every day, just two millionths of a gram. But that tiny amount keeps your central nervous system running smoothly, and a deficiency of this vitamin can lead to irreversible damage.

Vitamin B$_{12}$ occurs naturally in animal foods, so if you eat eggs or dairy products, you get plenty of it. There are no plant sources of vitamin B$_{12}$, but even if you are vegan, you can get it by eating foods fortified with B$_{12}$, such as certain breakfast cereals and some breads, pastas, and crackers. Just check the nutritional label, or write to the company for information (B$_{12}$ isn't always listed on the package). You can also get a reliable source of B$_{12}$ through Red Star T6635 nutritional yeast flakes, available

at natural food stores. People used to think that foods like tempeh, miso, and sea vegetables contained B_{12}, but they aren't reliable because they contain a lot of an inactive form that your
body can't use. If you aren't sure that you're getting B_{12} in the
foods you eat, take a supplement.

Here's where you can find a few other important nutrients:

VITAMIN A: *In yellow, orange, and dark-green
fruits and veggies, and in fortified low-fat milk
products and fortified soymilk.*

VITAMIN D: *From fortified low-fat milk products
or fortified soymilk, or from exposure to the sun.*

OTHER B VITAMINS: *(B_1 [thiamin], B_2 [ribo-
flavin], B_3 [niacin], B_6 [pyridoxine], and folic acid).
In whole-grain foods, vegetables, legumes, nuts,
low-fat milk products, and in foods fortified with B
vitamins (check the labels).*

ZINC: *In garbanzo beans, black-eyed peas, lentils,
lima beans, green peas, fortified cereals, oatmeal,
brown rice, wheat germ, pumpkin seeds, nuts, and
low-fat milk.*

NUTRITION IN YOUR EVERYDAY LIFE (OR, HOW TO MAKE SENSE OF ALL OF THIS)

Variety Is the Key

Eating a variety of foods will keep your diet interesting and
keep you healthy. Many people don't have a varied diet. Suppose the only vegetable you eat is corn. Corn is a wonderful

food. But if you eat only corn, you're missing the nutrients in other foods. The more varied your diet, the better your chances of covering all the nutritional bases.

Dietitians suggest a couple of tricks to add variety to your diet:

1. Eat foods of various colors. If your diet is bland in color, it's probably bland in nutrients. Paint a nutritious plate with (to name a few):

> **ORANGE FOODS:** *Sweet potatoes, squash, oranges, peaches, dried apricots.*
>
> **GREEN FOODS:** *Spinach, kale, collard greens, broccoli, green beans, peas.*
>
> **YELLOW FOODS:** *Bananas, yellow bell peppers, corn and corn tortillas, garbanzo beans, split peas.*
>
> **RED FOODS:** *Tomatoes, red bell peppers, apples.*
>
> **BURGUNDY FOODS:** *Red beans, kidney beans.*
>
> **PURPLISH FOODS:** *Black beans, berries, eggplant, grapes, plums, purple peppers, even purple potatoes!*
>
> **BROWN/BEIGE FOODS:** *Whole-wheat bread, veggie burgers, brown rice, tempeh, lentils, raisins, figs.*
>
> **WHITE FOODS:** *Tofu, low-fat cottage cheese, ricotta cheese.*

2. Discover ethnic foods. Different cultures include ingredients that you might otherwise miss out on. Remember, most of the world eats a primarily vegetarian diet, so you can find lots of vegetarian options at ethnic restaurants. Here's just a sample of the variety you'll find when you experiment with meals from around the world:

MEXICAN FOOD *features pinto beans and black beans, corn tortillas, avocados, rice, cilantro, and limes. Try burritos, tacos, tostadas, and beans and rice.*

INDIAN FOOD *contains chickpeas, cauliflower, eggplant, basmati rice, and mangoes. Try* dal *(split-pea soup),* aloo gobhi *(potato and cauliflower), and vegetable* samosas *(stuffed pastries). (Vegans note: Many Indian dishes contain* ghee, *or clarified butter.)*

THAI FOOD *offers you rice noodles, peanuts, mushrooms, tofu, and sweet basil. A favorite Thai dish is the noodle-y* pad Thai. *It's usually made with eggs and sometimes shrimp, but restaurants will leave those things out, if you ask.*

CHINESE FOOD *contains tofu and noodles, as well as snow peas, bok choy, and other fresh vegetables. Try vegetable noodle dishes like chow mein or lo mein, for starters.*

ETHIOPIAN FOOD *is made up of flat bread, split peas, lentils, cabbage, and spinach. Just tell your waiter that you want enough vegetarian food to feed the number at your table, and you'll be in for a tasty surprise.*

ITALIAN FOOD *is full of pasta and tomatoes, of course, with cheese if you want it. For a switch from pasta, try risotto, a creamy dish made from rice.*

JAPANESE FOOD *will introduce you to sea vegetables, miso, and shiitake mushrooms. Try vegetarian sushi rolls, made without fish.*

MIDDLE EASTERN FOOD *features chickpeas, eggplant, and sesame. Things to try include falafel (chickpea patty) sandwiches,* baba ganouj *(eggplant dip), and hummus (chickpea dip).*

Note: Mexican restaurants sometimes use lard in the refried beans, Chinese restaurants sometimes flavor vegetable dishes with pork or meat broth, and Thai restaurants sometimes use fish paste in curried dishes. Ask about nonvegetarian ingredients; often the cook can leave them out.

AVOIDING THE COMMON PITFALLS

Do You Eat Too Much Junk Food?

An order of fries every now and then isn't going to kill you. But when every day starts looking like this—a doughnut for breakfast; french fries, a candy bar, and soda for lunch; and greasy fast-food pizza for dinner—it's time to rethink your menu. What's wrong with so much junk food? For one thing, it has a lot of fat, but little good stuff. And eating so much junk food fills you up and takes the place of more nutritious things in your diet.

Do You Eat Too Few Fruits and Vegetables?

Okay, so you eat an occasional apple and maybe even a baked potato every week or so. Shoot for more: Try for four servings of fruits and four of vegetables every day.

Are You a Cheesehead? (Or Egghead?)

Have you replaced all the meat in your diet with cheese or eggs? Cheese omelettes for breakfast, grilled-cheese sandwich for lunch, cheese lasagna for dinner ... Whoa! A certain amount of dairy products can be healthy, but don't go overboard. Eggs and many milk products are high in fat and protein, but lack much of the good stuff in whole grains, fruits, and vegetables. For filling fare, try hot grain cereals, bean burritos, veggie and tofu stir-fries, or some of the great fakey meat products available.

PUTTING IT ALL TOGETHER

How can you, a teenage vegetarian, follow today's recommended nutrition guidelines and get all the nutrients you need? Every day, eat:

8 servings of **grains**, such as breads, pasta, rice, cereal, or other grains.

> Example: 1 slice bread
>
> ½ cup cooked grain or pasta

2 servings of **legumes**, such as split peas, lentils, black beans, chickpeas, or soyfoods like tofu or tempeh.

> Example: ½ cup of cooked beans
>
> 4 ounces of tofu or tempeh
>
> 1 tofu burger or hot dog

3 servings of *fortified* **low-fat soymilk** or **cow's milk.***

*You can also try Vegelicious, a powdered nondairy, nonsoy drink that you mix up yourself.

Example: 1 cup of low-fat soymilk or cow's milk

1½ ounces of low-fat soy cheese or dairy cheese

1 cup low-fat soy or dairy yogurt

4 servings of **vegetables**, such as dark leafy greens, broccoli, cauliflower, potatoes, carrots, or green peas.

Example: ½ cup cooked kale or broccoli

1 cup raw vegetables

1 medium baked potato

4 servings of **fruits**, such as banana, apple, pear, strawberries, or melon.

Example: 1 banana or apple

1 cup strawberries

1 serving **nuts** or **seeds**, such as almonds, sesame seeds, tahini (sesame paste), or other nut butters.

Example: 1 Tbs. sesame seeds

2 Tbs. almonds

2 Tbs. tahini

These guidelines give you plenty of leeway to include the foods that you like best, and the diet can be vegetarian or vegan. One final note: If you don't eat dairy or foods that are fortified with vitamin B_{12}, take a B_{12} supplement.

SO, WHAT'S ON THE MENU?

People may think vegetarians eat nothing but salad, but as you'll see, the menu possibilities are endless. Here's one way you could eat your way through any given day:

Breakfast:	*Food Group*
Bowl of fortified whole-grain cereal	grain
1 cup of low-fat soymilk or cow's milk	legume or dairy
1 glass of grapefruit juice	fruit
1 slice of whole-wheat toast with	grain
1 Tbs. tahini (sesame paste) or peanut butter	seed or nut

Snack:	
Banana	fruit
Handful of raisins	fruit

Lunch:	
1 tofu burger	legume
1 burger bun	grain
Toppings of tomato, lettuce, onion	vegetable
½ cup coleslaw	vegetable
Whole-grain crackers	grain
1 orange	fruit

Snack:	
Bagel with	grain
1 Tbs. peanut or cashew butter	nut

Dinner:	
Vegetarian chili made with beans,	legume
macaroni, tomato sauce,	grain
green pepper, onion	vegetable
Cornbread	grain
Sautéed kale	vegetable
Fresh lemonade	fruit
Low-fat soy yogurt or dairy yogurt	legume or dairy

Snack:

Graham crackers with jam	grain
1 cup of low-fat soymilk or cow's milk	legume or dairy

Notice what's happening in this menu: There's a lot of variety and you get high-iron and high-calcium foods, plus plenty of vitamin C. And all this was done without a lot of hocus-pocus, mixing, measuring, or calculating. Here's another menu:

Breakfast:

	Food Group
Scrambled tofu with	legume
green peppers and onions,	vegetable
sprinkled with sesame seeds	seed
2 slices rye toast	grain
Slice of melon	fruit
Herb tea	

Snack:

Pear	fruit
Wheat crackers	grain

Lunch:

Pita sandwich stuffed with	grain
sautéed kale	vegetable
1 cup raspberries	fruit
Carrot sticks	vegetable
1 cup low-fat soymilk or cow's milk	legume or dairy
Fruit spritzer	

Snack:

Bagel, spread with	grain
tahini and jam	seed

Dinner:

Burrito in flour tortilla with	grain
black beans, tomato, lettuce	legume, vegetable
Low-fat soy cheese or dairy cheese	legume or dairy
Rice	grain
Sliced peaches	fruit

Snack:

Banana-mango milkshake made with	fruit
low-fat soymilk or dairy milk	legume or dairy
Handful of cereal	grain

MEANWHILE, BACK IN THE REAL WORLD...

Okay. What's all this talk about strange new foods? Kale? Collard greens? Figs? Tempeh? "I could never be a vegetarian," some people say. "I could never learn to eat tofu." But one great thing about a vegetarian diet is that there are so many foods to try and so many ways to prepare them; if you don't like one thing, there's always something else. You don't like tofu? Don't eat tofu, but give tempeh a shot. If you think collard greens are gross, sample another dark leafy green instead. The point is that you'll be doing your body a favor if you at least *try* to take advantage of the abundance out there.

The truth is, when you're out in the "real world," you won't always be able to put together the totally perfect menu. But you can still make reasonably good choices, no matter where you are.

At School

If you don't want to take brown-bag lunches to school, what can you eat from the cafeteria? If there's a salad bar, go for that, and pile on the vegetables and beans. (Talk to your food-service director if there aren't enough nutritious items at the bar.) Some schools offer cheese pizza, which might be greasy, but okay every so often. Yogurt can be a good choice, but if it's the frozen variety, it's probably mostly sugar and fat. Other options: Ask for a double helping of vegetable side dishes from the cafeteria (skip the deep-fried stuff). Drink juice with your meal. If necessary, round out your meal with a snack from home, such as a bagel or crackers with bean dip.

Eating Out

Your best nutrition bets at fast-food restaurants include salads, baked potatoes, bean burritos, soft bean tacos, "burger-less" burgers, and vegetarian pizza. When at a full-service restaurant with no veggie entrée on the menu, ask for a baked potato and a good-sized salad. Another option: Request a plate of steamed veggies, perhaps with an order of pasta (get it plain if all the sauce is meaty, and then mix it with the veggies and a little dressing). Be creative!

WHAT YOU CAN DO

● Size up your diet. One way to identify areas where you can improve your diet is to keep a food diary. For about a week, write down everything you eat. Are you eating lots of fruits and vegetables? Do you eat too many eggs, too much cheese, too much junk food? Does your diet include plenty of calcium- and iron-rich foods? Make adjustments to give your diet a nutritional boost.

● Ask an expert. If you wonder whether something is missing from your diet, find out. The American Dietetic Association can help direct you to a dietitian in your area who is familiar with vegetarian diets. Call the ADA's nutrition hotline at (800) 366-1655.

● If your health class doesn't include a discussion on vegetarian nutrition, bring it up. It's something your teacher may want to cover along with the regular nutrition chapter in your textbook. You can offer to make posters to illustrate the lecture.

● Want more information? The Vegetarian Resource Group offers a straightforward pamphlet called "Vegetarian Nutrition for Teenagers." Send a self-addressed stamped envelope to VRG, Box 1463, Baltimore, MD 21203.

● Experiment! Try some new foods. This week, taste some black beans to see how you like them. Next week, try kale. After that, try eating brown rice or whole-wheat bread instead of the white, overprocessed varieties. Don't worry if you don't like everything you try; just move on to something else. Pretty soon, you'll be familiar with a whole new world of foods.

WHEN A VEGETARIAN DIET IS A SIGN OF SOMETHING UNHEALTHY

For most people, becoming a vegetarian is a positive step toward better health, or a way to live with compassion for the world around them. But there are some people who become vegetarian to disguise something dangerously wrong, namely an eating disorder.

People with eating disorders such as anor-

exia nervosa or bulimia nervosa typically make up rules for themselves to control or restrict their food intake. Some people will become vegetarians just to eliminate whole categories of foods from their diets. Meat and dairy products are things that people with eating disorders often want to eliminate because of their high fat and calorie contents. This practice becomes especially dangerous when a person judges her self-worth by how well she can stick to the "rules" of her diet. (Most, but not all, people with eating disorders are girls and women.) Sometimes a person with an eating disorder will start calling herself a vegetarian simply to avoid questions about why she won't eat certain things.

Of course, many people become vegetarian to lose a few pounds but never develop an eating disorder. How can you distinguish between a "real" vegetarian and one with a problem? If you're worried about yourself or someone you know, you can ask a few questions, for starters:

Why am I a vegetarian? Is it to get thin? Or do I have other reasons?

Am I obsessed with eating low-fat foods?

Do I feel guilty, like a failure, or somehow less than perfect if I eat meat, dairy products, or other high-fat vegetarian foods such as peanut butter or avocados? Do I feel like I have lost control?

Do I always feel fat?

Do I ever fast or go on really restrictive diets?

Do I have a ritual, where I eat the same foods every day?

Am I preoccupied with food? Will I fix it for others but not eat it myself?

An eating disorder is a serious problem that can lead to illness or even death. If you are concerned about yourself or a friend, please get help. For counseling, referrals, and information, contact Anorexia Nervosa and Related Eating Disorders, Inc. (ANRED), P.O. Box 5102, Eugene, OR 97405; (503) 344-1144.

CHAPTER 11

FABULOUS VEGETARIAN FOODS

*" The happiest person in the grocery store is the vegetarian
looking at the prices in the meat department. "*
—Ann Landers, "Gem of the Day"

~~~~~~~ "People think there's nothing to eat if you
don't eat meat," says Tennille Teague, 16. But a vegetarian diet
is hardly boring or bland. As you explore the world of vegetarian foods, your diet will become more exciting than it ever was
before. Try some of these:

GREAT GRAINS

Grains are things like rice, oats, and barley. Foods made with
grains include: bread, pasta, muffins, cookies, crackers, and

rice cakes. Grain foods are the foundation for many vegetarian meals. Grains are easy to cook, versatile, and are packed with nutrients. Whole grains are always better than the refined kind because they still have their really nutritious parts intact. (In other words, choose brown rice or whole-wheat bread over the white varieties.) You can find flour made from all different kinds of grain in your natural food store. Here are some great grains to try:

AMARANTH: *Nutty, sweet, and sticky, it's good as a hot cereal or in puddings.*

BARLEY: *Mild-tasting and chewy. Great in soups and salads.*

BUCKWHEAT: *Has a hearty, toasty taste that goes well with mushrooms and onions.*

CORN: *Cornbread, made with cornmeal, is super-easy to make and great with soup or chili.*

KAMUT *(pronounced kah-MOOT):* *Rich and satisfying flavor. You can buy kamut cereal, bread, and pasta.*

MILLET: *A small, round grain that's great for stuffing bell peppers and other vegetables, or as a hot breakfast cereal.*

OATS: *Oats are tasty for breakfast and also in baked goods. Add to banana bread or muffins in place of some of the flour.*

PASTA: *Pasta is a grain product, but so versatile, yummy, and easy to prepare that it deserves its own special mention. For fun's sake, look beyond plain old spaghetti. There's rotini (twisty pasta), penne (quill-shaped pasta), wagon wheels, orzo (looks like rice),* *shells, ramen noodles, Japanese buckwheat soba noodles, and herb noodles (mmm, lemon-pepper fettucine . . .). People who are allergic to wheat (a not-uncommon problem, according to some nutritionists) can get pasta made from corn, rice, or kamut.*

QUINOA *(pronounced KEEN-wah):* A supernutritious grain that you can top with stir-fried vegetables or use in a cold grain salad.

RICE: *Brown rice comes in all lengths and varieties. For a real treat, try basmati rice, a sweet, nutty-tasting rice that's good with Indian and Thai foods.*

SPELT: *Tastes sort of like whole wheat, but a little lighter.*

TEFF: *This little grain has a slight chocolate flavor. Try some hot for breakfast.*

WHEAT: *Wheat is everywhere: in breads, pastas, you name it. If you bake, experiment with whole-wheat flour or whole-wheat pastry flour, or a blend of whole-wheat and unbleached white flour in your recipes. Try these wheat products too: bulgur (a type of cracked wheat that's used to make tabouli, a Middle Eastern grain salad), and couscous (sort of like pasta broken up into tiny, tiny pieces). Both cook really fast and can be used instead of rice.*

BEANS, BEANS, BEANS

If you've been thinking that your parents won't let you be a vegetarian because it costs too much, then you don't know beans. Literally, you must not know about beans. Dried beans are super-inexpensive. But that's not the only reason you might want to try them. Beans (also called legumes) are just about the perfect food, nutritionally speaking—they're high in protein, iron, and fiber, and contain almost zero fat. You can use them in just about everything: in soups, salads, burritos, over rice, and made into dips and sandwich spreads. If you've never cooked a batch of beans from scratch before, don't be intimidated. Turn to page 158 for some basic measures and cooking times. If that sounds too tough, buy your beans canned. Try these:

BLACK BEANS: *Great in burritos and chili.*

BLACK-EYED PEAS: *Popular in southern and soul food.*

GARBANZO BEANS (OR CHICKPEAS): *Mash them up and make some hummus, or sprinkle them onto salads.*

KIDNEY BEANS: *A staple in chili and cold bean salads.*

LENTILS: *The fastest-cooking beany thing around. Yumm-o with a touch of olive oil in soups and stews.*

PINTO BEANS: *Refry them or leave them whole for burritos.*

SPLIT PEAS: *The green kind make the classic split-pea soup. Try yellow ones in an Indian soup called dal.*

WHITE BEANS: *Navy beans and great northern beans are perfect in hearty veggie stews and soups.*

Also experiment with a few of the wacky-sounding bean varieties, like rattlesnake beans or the New Mexico appaloosa.

SUPER SOYFOODS

Can you believe that the following foods all come from the little soybean?

TOFU: *What exactly is that jiggly white stuff?
Tofu, or bean curd, is sort of like a cheese: Milk made
from soybeans is hardened into blocks with a mineral salt. (Note: Tofu that's hardened with calcium
sulfate or calcium chloride will supply the most calcium to your diet.) Plain tofu doesn't taste like much
to most people (although some love it right out of
the package!), but tofu picks up the flavor of whatever you mix it with. You can use it to make so many
great things. Different types of tofu work best in certain types of recipes: Extra-firm and firm styles of
tofu are great cubed in stir-fries, stews, and potpies,
or sliced, marinated, and baked for sandwiches. You
can even grill it at your next barbecue. (You can
make firm tofu even firmer by wrapping it in a
towel and pressing all the water out of it. You can
make it chewier and "meatier" by freezing it and
then thawing it. It's good this way crumbled into
chili.) Soft and silken styles of tofu are perfect ingredients in dressings, desserts, and fruit smoothies.
You can also substitute tofu for eggs in some baked
goods.*

Tofu is rich in protein, iron, and calcium. It also

contains a fair amount of fat, but this won't be a problem if you balance your diet with veggies and grains. You can also buy reduced-fat tofu.

TEMPEH: *Tempeh, a staple food in Indonesia, is even stranger-looking than tofu. It looks like a little cake of soybeans that have been glued together. Actually, tempeh is made by fermenting soybeans with a friendly bacteria that basically weaves the beans together. Like tofu, tempeh soaks up the flavor of whatever you season it with. You can make a quick tempeh sandwich: Slice tempeh into patties and sauté in oil or water, soy sauce, garlic, and seasoning (try curry powder—yum!). Also good for shish kebabs, or in stews or stir-fries.*

SOYMILK: *Soymilk is a fun beverage to try. It comes in lots of flavors, like vanilla, chocolate, and carob. Even the plain flavor is sweeter than dairy milk, so if you're looking for a soymilk that tastes the most like dairy milk, pick the plain flavor in one of the "light" varieties. Flavors vary from brand to brand, so experiment. Also, read the labels and choose a soymilk that's low-fat and fortified with calcium and vitamin D.*

You can use soymilk any way you would cow's milk: over cereal, in baked goods (it helps them rise a little bit), or just by the glass. About the only drawback of soymilk is the packaging: It comes in aseptic boxes made from a blend of materials that's tricky to recycle. You can call the Aseptic Packaging Council at (800) 277-8088 to locate a recycling program in your area that accepts aseptic boxes.

Note: While you're sampling the soymilks, don't overlook other dairy-milk alternatives. You'll find rice milk and almond beverages at your natural food store, too. For a real treat, try amazake, a thick, sweet, milkshake-like drink made from cultured rice.

SOY CHEESE: *Use soy cheese however you would regular cheese. (At Leona's restaurant in Chicago, they even make a super-thick stuffed pizza out of it.) Soy cheese comes in many varieties, such as ched-dar, mozzarella, Monterey jack, and jalepeño jack. Also look for reduced-fat varieties (some soy cheeses contain quite a bit of fat). Soy cheese doesn't melt as well as dairy cheese, but it does melt. The reason it melts is that most manufacturers add a dairy deriv-ative called casein to the soy cheese. If that's not cool with you, read the labels and look for the few vari-eties made without casein.*

MORE SOY GOODIES: *There are soyfoods to mimic nearly every dairy food: soy ice creams (and rice-based ones, too), soy yogurts, soy sour cream, soy cream cheese, soy salad dressings, and soy mayon-naise. Try them!*

MISO *(pronounced MEE-soh): A salty, fermen-ted paste made from soybeans and grains, miso comes in many varieties. It has been referred to as the beef bouillon of vegetarian cooking because it adds such rich flavoring to soup stocks, sauces, gravies, and spreads. Dark-colored miso is* *much stronger-tasting than the lighter-colored varieties, which are actually quite mild and sweet.*

TAMARI *(pronounced ta-MAR-ee): A naturally brewed soy sauce, with a special salty/sweet/savory flavor. Try a splash over vegetables and rice.*

FABULOUS FRUITS AND VEGGIES

Next time you go grocery shopping with your folks, explore the produce section. Get to know some new items.

BOK CHOY: *Add this Chinese cabbage to your favorite stir-fry.*

DRIED FRUITS: *Dried apricots and figs have lots of iron and they're easy to carry around in your backpack for a quick snack. Try dried bananas, dried papaya, and dried pineapple.*

EGGPLANT: *Slice into rounds, brush with Italian dressing, and grill.*

KALE: *Steam or sauté and drizzle with a light vinaigrette dressing. This works well with collard and chard, too.*

KUMQUATS: *They look like miniature oranges, and you can eat them whole—skin and all (look for organic ones).*

LEEKS: *Add some to soups for a mild, oniony flavor.*

MANGOES: *Blend mango pulp with low-fat soy or dairy yogurt for a sweet, refreshing drink.*

POMEGRANATES: *One of the most fun fruits to eat. Peel the skin and pop the juicy seeds right into your mouth. Tart!*

RHUBARB: *Makes an incredible pie or baked crisp.*

SPROUTS: *Add fresh flavor and crunch to sandwiches and salads. Try zesty radish or onion sprouts.*

SQUASH: *Stuff it with seasoned bread crumbs and bake; add a sprinkling of soy or dairy cheese. For dessert: Fill baked squash with a scoop of ice cream and drizzle with maple syrup.*

SWEET POTATOES: *Microwave whole and eat like you would a regular baked potato.*

NUTTY NUTS AND SEEDS

Nuts and seeds pack protein, vitamins, and minerals into your diet. Pumpkin, sesame, and sunflower seeds have lots of calcium. All nuts (except chestnuts) are also high in fat. You can add nuts to your diet by toasting and sprinkling them over your favorite foods. One really tasty seed blend is called *gomasio,* which is toasted, ground sesame seeds combined with a little bit of salt (good over stir-fried veggies). Try nut butters and seed pastes, too. Sure, there's peanut butter, but almond butter and cashew butter are super-yummy. One versatile seed paste to keep on hand is tahini, or sesame paste. It's used in Middle Eastern foods like hummus and in sauce that you pour over falafel. It's great spread on toast with honey or jam for a quick breakfast or snack.

DAIRY PRODUCTS

If you love dairy products, choose low-fat varieties, like skim milk instead of whole. For variety, choose these:

LOW-FAT RICOTTA CHEESE: *Good as filling in veggie lasagna or stuffed shell pasta.*

LOW-FAT YOGURT: *Blended with fresh fruit, makes a filling snack.*

ORGANIC CHEESE: *From cows that haven't been fed or treated with chemical pesticides, fertilizers, or hormones. One brand to look for is North Farm Co–op. It comes in many varieties.*

MORE WACKY WONDERFUL FOODS

TEXTURED VEGETABLE PROTEIN (TVP®): *Not a very friendly name, but a really cool food. TVP is made from soy flour that has had the oil removed. It comes dry in tiny granules, flakes, and chunks, and when you add boiling water, it turns very meat-like. You could substitute TVP for meat in things like chili and tacos and fool your friends. You can buy TVP at a natural food store, or order it from the Mail Order Catalog, P.O. Box 180, Summertown, TN 38483; (800) 695-2241.*

SEITAN *(pronounced SAY-tan):* *Another weird name for another wild food. Seitan is also called "wheat meat," and that's exactly what it is: a meat-like food made from wheat flour kneaded with water, rolled into a roast shape, and boiled. Depending on how it's sliced and seasoned, it can* *take the place of chicken, beef, even barbecued ribs. In fact, some vegetarians think it's too meat-like, but if you taste it, you'll see that it really has its own subtle flavor. You can buy chunks of seitan bottled in seasoned broth, frozen seitan formed and seasoned (take some seitan burgers to your next barbecue), or as a dry mix to cook up yourself. You can also make it from scratch, but it takes several hours.*

SEA VEGETABLES: *Sea vegetables are loaded with nutrients, including calcium, iron, and potassium. Choose from: arame, dulse, hijiki, kombu and wakame, and also nori, which is what's wrapped around rice and vegetables to make vegetarian sushi. Yes, it's seaweed. But seaweed really isn't all that strange. It's found in many ice cream products, including fast-food milkshakes. And, as humor columnist Cecil Adams put it: "Every McDonald's hamburger contains pieces of—brace yourself— dead cow. So let's not get hung up on a little seaweed."*

NUTRITIONAL YEAST: *Not the same kind of yeast you would use to make bread rise. Nutritional yeast comes in flake form and has a golden color and a sort of cheesy taste. It's really good sprinkled over popcorn, pasta, and other dishes, and it can be made into gravy and sauces. (One brand of fortified nutritional yeast, Red Star T6635, contains vitamin B_{12}, but other nutritional yeasts and brewer's yeasts do not.)*

EGG REPLACER: *If you want to give up eggs but not baking, you can use powdered egg replacer for the eggs in your cakes, cookies, and muffins. Buy something called ENER-G Egg Replacer in natural food stores. It's made from potato starch, tapioca flour, and other ingredients.*

OTHER GREAT PRODUCTS TO KNOW ABOUT

- *Instant vegetarian meals-in-a-cup (you add water)*
- *Boxed tofu meal mixes (add tofu to premixed seasonings)*
- *Frozen vegetarian TV dinners (hey, no one likes to cook all of the time)*
- *Veggie burgers (boxed mixes and premade, frozen patties)*
- *Tofu dogs (take them to a cookout)*
- *Fake lunch meat (made from seitan)*
- *Fruit juice spritzers (try them instead of soda)*

WHAT YOU CAN DO

- Plan ahead. Before shopping for new foods, check out some vegetarian cookbooks from the library and browse through them. Foods will look less confusing if you can picture them as part of actual meals.
- Be adventuresome. Sure, some of these foods sound weird. But give them a shot. "I always like to try something at least once," says Jessica, 15.

WHERE DO I GET THIS STUFF?

"Wait a minute," you're thinking. "My local store doesn't carry tempeh or soymilk." You can be a vegetarian and shop only at a supermarket. But supermarkets don't always sell some of the more unusual foods you might want to try. Where can you find them?

- *Natural food stores contain lots of foods that were made just for vegetarians. Some things in natural food stores are kind of expensive, but you can find some really good deals there, too. (To find a natural food store in your area, look up "Health food store" in the Yellow Pages.) Natural food stores come in all sizes and styles. On one end of the spectrum are tiny shops that sell mostly vitamins and powdered meal mixes for athletes. On the other end are the supermarket-sized stores that have aisles and aisles of food and even in-store cafés. Most are somewhere in the middle, with a good selection of packaged foods and organic produce.*

- *Ethnic groceries often sell lots of great vegetarian foods—soyfoods, vegetables, and spices, for instance—for really good prices. If you live in a multicultural community, be sure to explore the Asian, Indian, Hispanic, and African markets.*

- *Farmers' markets are great places to get cheap, often organic, fresh fruits and vegetables.*

- *You can also shop by mail. You can have many vegetarian foods delivered right to your home through a mail-order food company. Check out the resources listed in the back of the book.*

WHAT A BARGAIN! *Your parents might say they can't afford to feed you a special diet. Sure, you could ring up a big grocery bill if you bought lots of premade, prepackaged vegetarian convenience foods all the time. But many vegetarian staples are the cheapest foods around. Dried beans and grains are super-cheap, especially when you buy them in bulk. Fruits and vegetables are always on sale. Besides, your family will buy less meat once you become a vegetarian. Meat can be pricey, and you also pay for bones and other parts you don't use. Tempeh and tofu are inexpensive, and there's no waste.*

GO ORGANIC! *It's always better to buy organic produce instead of the regular stuff. It might cost more, but think about the savings to the planet: Organic growing methods are better for the environment, farmworkers, and your own health. If organic food is available, go for it.*

CHAPTER 12

THE MAKINGS OF A MEAL

❝It's nice to eat a meal and not have to worry about what your food may have died of. ❞

—Harvey Kellogg, M.D.,
originator of ready-to-eat breakfast cereals

Back in the good old days, when you asked "What's for dinner?" you heard the evening's menu. Now you'll hear something like "We're having chicken. What are you eating?" Some parents just have no idea what to make for their vegetarian kids. As one teen plainly puts it: "You're probably going to have to start cooking some meals for yourself."

What do you do? What if you have no idea how to create a meal? What if you don't even know how to cook? Well, you could survive on peanut butter and jelly sandwiches, cheese pizza, and spaghetti with bottled sauce. But that'll get old after a while. And nutritionally, you can do a lot better. If you're going to pull this off (and show your family that you're serious), you might want to do a little research, and maybe even turn on the oven.

But relax. There are plenty of helpful resources for you to turn to. Your local library and bookstores are brimming with wonderful vegetarian cookbooks that can inspire you and teach you some cooking basics. There might even be a vegetarian cooking course in your area (ask your local natural food store). But you don't have to spend a lot of time or money to figure out how to feed yourself. This chapter contains some tips on putting together easy, nutritious meals.

GET OUT OF THE MEAT-AS-MAIN-COURSE MODE

First things first. Before you can start cooking and eating like a vegetarian, start thinking like one. Most of us grow up thinking of meat as the main course. But try thinking instead of vegetables, fruits, grains, and beans as wonderful, filling, nutritious foods—not just as side dishes. If you can do that, you can create many satisfying meals. Try these ideas as entrées. You can make most of them with what's already in the kitchen.

PASTA: *Don't stop at tomato sauce as a topper. Add fresh or frozen vegetables, cooked beans, tofu, or even a sprinkling of nuts. Anything you want. "For lunch today, I had pasta and kale," says Chy Lin.*

GRAINS: *Top a bed of rice, millet, or couscous with vegetables in sauce, or cooked beans.*

POTATOES: *Top a baked white or sweet potato with a grain and vegetables, or seasoned cooked beans.*

SALADS: *Beans, tofu, or cheese on top of a green salad turn it into something filling. Try making a grain salad by mixing cooked quinoa, couscous, or rice with cut-up veggies, garbanzo beans, and your favorite dressing.*

BEANS: *Hearty bean soup or chili can be a meal in itself. For quick burritos, roll up whole beans with rice and vegetables. "I'll make a huge pot of beans and eat those all week," says John.*

BREAKFAST FOODS: *Don't eat them just in the morning. Keep a whole-grain pancake mix on hand and make a batch for dinner. Roll 'em up with steamed vegetables and a sprinkling of cheese or light dressing.*

ETHNIC FARE: *Tostadas, chop suey, dal (a kind of soup), and eggplant parmigiana are just a few.*

FAKE YOURSELF OUT! *If you can't get away from the idea of a meatlike main course, try one of the many meat substitutes on the market, or make your own. "I eat a lot of veggie burgers," says one teen.*

THE VEGETARIAN LUNCH BAG

No good choices in your school cafeteria? "I take lunch from home to school," says Carrie. Here are some ideas:

Pack a Pita

Pita bread is a great holder for sandwich fillings that might otherwise fall out of regular bread. To keep your pita from getting soggy, pack fillings separately and fill sandwiches at school. Some good fillings include:

TOFU SALAD: *Crumble tofu, stir in finely chopped green pepper, green onions, carrots, a touch of curry powder, salt, and pepper (and a drop of olive oil if it seems dry).*

HUMMUS: *Top this chickpea dip with cucumbers, lettuce, and tomato.*

SNAZZY SALAD: *Start with a bed of greens and thinly sliced vegetables, sprinkle with cheese or cooked kidney beans, drizzle with low-oil dressing.*

BEAN SALAD: *Combine your favorite cooked beans with chopped green pepper, onion, or other vegetable. Add dressing, salt, and pepper. Top with tomato.*

BEAN SPREAD: *Mash up your favorite canned beans with seasonings. Use relish with baked beans, dill and soy mayonnaise with white beans, and salsa with pinto or black beans.*

Other Creative Sandwich Snacks

LIGHT CHEESE SPREAD: *Combine low-fat cottage or ricotta cheese with finely chopped red pepper, celery, and spices; spread on thick slices of bread.*

PB & BAGEL: *Mix together peanut butter (or other nut butter) and honey. Add mashed banana, if you please. Eat on a cinnamon-raisin or banana-nut bagel.*

TOMATO & BASIL: *Top a bagel or crusty bread with soy mayonnaise and a touch of chopped fresh basil. Add a thick slice of ripe tomato.*

More Mobile Lunches

PRESTO PASTA SALAD: *Cold pasta salad makes a filling lunch that you can pack in a reusable container. (You'll look so environmentally aware.) Toss cooked pasta spirals with chopped red bell pepper, black olives, onions, broccoli pieces, and green peas (or just use a frozen vegetable mix). Add premade, oil-free Italian dressing. Toss in cheese cubes, if you like, and sprinkle with salt and pepper.*

BURRITO ROLL-UP: *When you have burritos for dinner, make an extra and refrigerate it for tomorrow's lunch. A burrito is good on-the-go food because it's easy to transport, and you can eat it right out of your hand. Just wrap it up snugly so it stays together.*

VEGGIE BURGERS (OR DOGS): *Even supermarkets now sell meatless burgers (look for Harvest Burgers in the frozen section, next to the premade meat patties). Cook up a patty before school and top it with all the fixings.*

FREEZE-A-YOGURT: *If your school doesn't sell yogurt, you can pack your own. Just freeze the container overnight and pack it in your lunch bag (wrap it in a towel to absorb the moisture). It will be thawed but still cold by midday.*

SUPERFAST, ON-THE-RUN DINNERS

When you're really pressed for time, these tips can provide an alternative to the fries-and-Coke routine.

Try to keep a container of cooked grain (rice, millet, quinoa) in the fridge, cans of beans in the pantry, and frozen vegetables in the freezer. In minutes flat, you can scoop rice onto a plate, plop some black beans and broccoli on top, and throw the whole thing in a microwave to heat.

Cooked pasta is another good thing to stash in the refrigerator. Top noodles with bottled sauce, frozen peas or broccoli, and maybe a few chickpeas or a pinch of cheese. Microwave until heated.

Toss a potato into the microwave (pierce it with a fork first) and heat on high for about 8 to 10 minutes. Top with canned vegetarian chili or baked beans.

This one takes a little longer, but it's still fast (about 30 minutes). Top a premade pizza crust with ready-made pizza sauce and lots of vegetables: sliced zucchini, mushrooms, or frozen broccoli. Top with cheese if you'd like, but with enough vegetables you don't really need it.

For more superfast meal ideas, check out *Meatless Meals for Working People: Quick & Easy Vegetarian Recipes* by Debra Wasserman and Charles Stahler (Vegetarian Resource Group, 1991).

I'LL HAVE WHAT THEY'RE HAVING (OR, EATING IN SYNC WITH YOUR FAMILY)

You don't have to cook all your own meals from beginning to end. Sometimes, you can have what your family is having—

altered to fit your own vegetarian taste. Suppose an Italian meal is in the works. Before the cook slips meat into the sauce, ask if you can have some without it. If lasagna is on the menu, build a small vegetarian one on the side, using spinach and perhaps tofu instead of meat. The rest of the meal—bread, salad, etc.—should be edible.

Being a vegetarian doesn't require special tools. But if you have access to any of these, they can make cooking a lot easier:

HELPFUL KITCHEN TOOLS

SHARP, STURDY KNIFE & CUTTING BOARD: *For chopping all those vegetables.*

FOOD PROCESSOR: *For grinding up beans and nuts and making smooth dips and creamy soups.*

PRESSURE COOKER: *Cuts the cooking time of beans way down.*

ELECTRIC RICE COOKER: *You can put the rice on and not have to watch the pot.*

STEAMER BASKET: *For steaming vegetables.*

WOK: *For perfect stir-fries.*

TOASTER OVEN: *For grilling sandwiches and warming up little meals.*

WOODEN SPOONS: *They're sturdy and don't get hot during cooking.*

GO AHEAD: GRILL IT! *You might think that barbecues and vegetarians don't mix, but actually a barbecue is one of the easiest meatless meals to plan. You can grill veggie burgers, tofu dogs, thick slices of eggplant, corn on the cob, onion chunks, mushrooms, bell* *peppers—even fruit or slabs of bread. Make shish kebabs by skewering extra-firm tofu or tempeh cubes with vegetables; brush with a marinade or sauce. Ask if you can have a meat-free spot on the grill, or cover the grill with a bit of foil if you'd rather not get any meat residue on your dinner. You can also cook your food before or after the meat is on the grill.*

HOW TO COOK BEANS

For 1 cup of soaked beans, cooked in 3 to 4 cups of water.

Bean Type	Cooking Time
Black beans	1½ to 2 hours
Black-eyed peas	1 to 1½ hours
Garbanzos (chickpeas)	2½ to 3 hours
Great northern beans	1½ to 2 hours
Kidney beans	1½ to 2 hours
Lentils	30 to 45 minutes
Lima beans	1 to 1½ hours
Navy beans	2 to 2½ hours
Pinto beans	2 to 2½ hours
Red beans	2½ to 3 hours
Soybeans	3 hours or more
Split peas	30 to 45 minutes

Easy Bean Tips

- Sort through dried beans to remove stones or bad beans.
- Soak dried beans in two to three times their volume of water for eight hours or overnight. This helps them cook

faster and makes them more digestible. Cook them in fresh water, not soaking water. (Lentils and split peas don't need soaking.)

● Quick-soak method: Bring pot of beans and water to boil and cook for one minute. Turn off heat, cover, and let stand for two to three hours. Cook beans in fresh water.

● Beans cook much faster in a pressure cooker (in about one-third of the normal time), and you don't have to soak them. Follow the manufacturer's instructions.

● To make beans less gas-producing, you can: 1) Soak first and cook in fresh water. 2) Cook beans thoroughly. 3) Eat beans in small portions at first, giving your system time to adapt. 4) Try Beano or other gas-preventing product.

HOW TO COOK GRAINS

Grain Type	Cooking Time
Use 1 cup grain to 2 cups water for:	
Brown rice	45 minutes to 1 hour
Buckwheat (kasha)	15 minutes
Bulgur wheat	15 minutes in boiled water, heat off
Quinoa	15 minutes
Couscous	15 minutes in boiled water, heat off
Use 1 cup grain to 2½ to 3 cups water for:	
Amaranth	25 minutes
Barley (pearled)	45 minutes to 1 hour
Millet	40 minutes

Wild rice   1 hour or more

Use 1 cup grain to 4 cups water for:
Cornmeal   25 minutes

Easy Grain Tips

- Rinse grains (except rolled grains, like oat flakes) in a strainer before cooking.
- For a nutty flavor, toast grains in a dry or lightly oiled skillet before cooking.
- Boil water first and slowly stir in grain. Reduce heat, cover, and simmer until water is absorbed. Don't stir until grain is done. (Note: Bulgur and couscous don't even require simmering time. Just add to boiling water, turn off heat, and let sit until water is absorbed.) If grain is still too chewy, add a little extra water and simmer again.

GOOD THINGS TO HAVE ON HAND

These foods will help you throw meals together in a flash. Most are things your family probably already buys.

Canned tomatoes and tomato sauce
Canned beans
Pasta
Lentils
Quick-cooking brown rice
Whole-grain bread
Tortillas
Whole-grain cereal

Peanut and other nut butters

Tofu or tempeh

Low-fat dairy milk or soymilk

Low-fat cheese

Frozen vegetables and fruits

An assortment of produce

Dried fruit

Nuts

Olive oil

Vinegar

Canned or instant vegetable broth

Nutritional yeast

Soy sauce or tamari

HIDDEN ANIMAL INGREDIENTS

"At first it was kind of hard avoiding hidden meats and animal products in foods," says Fernando. "But I got used to reading labels." Keep your eyes open for these hidden animal ingredients:

ALBUMIN: *A substance usually derived from egg whites. Used to thicken or add texture to foods such as cereals, frostings, and puddings.*

ANCHOVIES: *These fish are an ingredient in almost all Worcestershire sauces and in Caesar salad.*

ANIMAL SHORTENING: *This is animal fat. Appears in cookies, crackers, snack cakes, and other processed foods.*

CARMINE COCHINEAL: *Red coloring from the body of an insect. Found in some juice, candy, and other processed foods.*

CASEIN: *A milk protein. Added to most soy cheeses to improve texture and make them melt. In other "nondairy" products, too. (Sometimes listed as "caseinate" on labels.)*

GELATIN: *Made from animal bones. Appears in lots of things: marshmallows, nonfat yogurts, even roasted peanuts. Note: "Kosher" gelatin is usually vegetarian; contact the company to make sure.*

LARD: *Another name for animal fat. Traditionally used in refried beans.*

NATURAL FLAVORINGS: *Depending on the product, these could include flavorings from meat.*

RENNET: *An enzyme from the lining of calves' stomachs. Used to make cheese. (Often just listed as "enzymes" on a cheese label. Look for "rennetless" cheese or cheese made with "vegetable enzymes.")*

WHEY: *Comes from milk. Found in many processed foods.*

Animal ingredients are everywhere. Shampoos may contain collagen, placenta, animal proteins, and keratin; most commercial soaps contain tallow from beef fat; some contact lens weekly cleaners contain pork enzymes. Animal ingredients are found in photographic and video film and in some makeup, laundry soaps, and kitchen cleansers. Some animal products are next to impossible to avoid—they're even used to make rubber tires and some upholstery fabric. The list goes on and on. The group People for the Ethical Treatment of Animals (PETA) can help you identify hidden animal ingredients. Write PETA, P.O. Box 42516, Washington, DC 20015.

WHAT YOU CAN DO

- Ask for a veggie cookbook for your next birthday present. (People will *know* you're serious about this vegetarian thing.)
- Experiment! Don't limit yourself to other people's recipes. If you think dried apricots and artichoke hearts would taste great in a salad, throw them in.
- Keep a file of your favorite recipes. Even a notebook is fine. You'll like having this resource to turn to when you just can't think of what to make for dinner.
- Share your creations. Offer to cook a meal for your friends or family. This is a great way to get them turned on to vegetarian fare.

EGG SUBSTITUTES   *Want to eliminate eggs from your favorite baked goods? Consider these possibilities. (You may need to experiment some to get good results.)*

- *Use ½ mashed banana or two ounces of mashed tofu for 1 egg in sweet baked goods.*
- *Add an extra ½ teaspoon baking powder and about 2 tablespoons extra liquid to a recipe to replace one egg.*
- *Use powdered egg replacer, such as Ener-G brand, available in natural food stores.*

CHAPTER 13

SOME RECIPES TO GET YOU STARTED

"We all love animals, but why do we call some pets and some dinner?"

—k. d. lang

~~~~~~~~~~Ready to hit the kitchen? There are count-less vegetarian cookbooks to help guide you, but here's a handful of recipes just to get you going: a few dinner ideas, a couple of lunch-box ideas, and even a sampling of animal-free sweets. Most of the recipes (except for the stir-fry, the burritos, the soup, and the sandwich spreads, which are from the author) were created by 17-year-old Sonnet Pierce, a veg-etarian who lives in rural Missouri. Sonnet does all of the

cooking for her family, and she writes all her own recipes. "I'm planning on being a vegetarian chef, and I'm working on a cookbook," she says. Sonnet cooks without eggs and dairy products, and she tries to keep everything low in fat. Sonnet's recipes often appear in the *How On Earth!* newsletter.

So let's get cooking!

DELICIOUS DINNERS

TOFU POTPIE

A warming, comforting dish that will remind you of chicken potpie. You can make it without tofu, too; just use an extra cup of vegetables.

Crust:

¾ cup barley flour or unbleached white flour (see note)

½ cup whole-wheat flour or whole-wheat pastry flour

½ tsp. salt

3 Tbs. oil

¼ cup water

Filling:

2½ cups vegetable broth (see note)

3 cups diced potato

1 cup finely chopped carrot

½ cup chopped onion

1 cup frozen green peas, corn kernels, or chopped celery
    (or combination of any of these equaling 1 cup)

½ cup chopped mushrooms (optional)

¼ cup flour

¼ tsp. pepper

½ tsp. poultry seasoning

½ cup soymilk or water (filling tastes much richer with
     soymilk)

1 package (10.5 oz. or 16 oz.) extra-firm tofu, cut into cubes
     (see note)

Salt to taste

Crust: Mix together flours and salt. Stir in oil, then mix in
water. Chill dough while making filling.

Filling: In a large saucepan, bring vegetable broth to a boil
over medium-high heat. Add potatoes, cover, and cook 5 minutes. Add carrot, onion, and celery (if using). Cover and cook 3
minutes. Add peas and/or corn and mushrooms (if using).
Cover and cook 2 minutes or until vegetables are tender.

In a small bowl, combine flour, pepper, and poultry seasoning. Add soymilk or water and beat together well. Gradually
add to vegetable mixture, stirring well. Over medium-high
heat, stir constantly for about 3 minutes, or until mixture is
thickened and bubbly. Remove from heat and stir in tofu
cubes. Add salt to taste.

To assemble: Heat oven to 350°. Using a rolling pin, roll
out dough to fit over the top of a medium-sized casserole dish (9" square, or something about that size). Spoon
tofu-vegetable mixture into casserole dish and cover with
crust, cutting off any extra dough and folding over and pinch-
ing edges to seal (you can make fancy markings along the
edges of the dough, if you want). Cut 4 or 5 slits on top of
dough to allow steam to escape. Bake for about 40 minutes,
or until crust is done. Let stand 10 minutes before serving.
Serves 6.

Note about flours: You can use pretty much whatever combination of flours you want (or all whole-wheat, or all unbleached white); just make sure the total flour amount equals 1¼ cups. Barley flour is available at natural food stores.

Note about the vegetable broth: You can buy canned vegetable broth (Swanson) at any supermarket. You can also find vegetable bouillon cubes or vegetable broth powder at a natural food store. Or check a vegetarian cookbook for a recipe for homemade vegetable broth.

Note about the tofu: For best results, drain liquid from tofu. Then wrap block of tofu in paper towels or a cloth and press out excess water before cubing.

SUPER SAUCY EGGPLANT LASAGNA

A great entrée for big gatherings. This lasagna is so full of texture and tang that no one will miss the meat or the cheese (in fact, some people might think the tofu *is* cheese). Of course, you can serve with a little grated cheese, if you'd like.

Sauce:

1 Tbs. olive oil

1 cup chopped onion

½ cup chopped bell pepper

4 cups finely diced peeled eggplant

1 cup sliced mushrooms

6 cups stewed tomatoes (with juice)

12 ounces tomato paste (2 small cans)

2 tsp. granulated garlic (or 2 cloves fresh pressed garlic)

2 tsp. dried or fresh basil

½ tsp. salt (optional)

1 tsp. dried oregano

½ tsp. dried thyme

¼ tsp. ground black pepper

2 Tbs. brown sugar

2 Tbs. tamari or soy sauce

Tofu filling:

1 package (10.5 oz. or 16 oz.) soft or silken tofu

1 Tbs. nutritional yeast

¼ tsp. granulated garlic

¼ tsp. salt

1 lb. lasagna noodles, cooked and drained

Sauce: In a heavy 4-quart saucepan or Dutch oven, sauté onion in olive oil for 1 minute. Add pepper and sauté 1 minute more. Add eggplant, cover, and cook on medium heat for 5 minutes, stirring often. Add some of the tomato juice, if necessary, to avoid sticking. Add mushrooms and cook 1 minute, uncovered. Stir in stewed tomatoes, tomato paste, garlic, basil, salt (if using), oregano, thyme, pepper, brown sugar, and tamari or soy sauce. Cook over low heat until hot.

Filling: In a small bowl, mash tofu with yeast, garlic, and salt, using a fork, until the mixture is the consistency of cottage cheese.

To assemble: Heat oven to 350°. Put a layer of noodles in a lightly oiled 12 x 16" pan (or pan of equivalent size). Cover with a generous layer of sauce. Repeat, this time putting half of the tofu over the sauce. Continue layering noodles and sauce, putting remaining tofu on top. Bake lasagna for 15–20 minutes or until hot. Serves 8 to 10.

EASY SESAME-BROCCOLI STIR-FRY

It practically takes as little time to make this dish as it does to order out for Chinese food. The broccoli and sesame seeds provide lots of calcium.

2 Tbs. tamari

1 tsp. sweet soy sauce or brown sugar (see note)

3 Tbs. cornstarch

1 cup water

2 tsp. to 1 Tbs. sesame oil

4 to 6 cloves garlic, pressed

8 cups broccoli pieces

½ cup chopped mushrooms (optional)

Black pepper

Sesame seeds

Cooked white or brown rice

In a small bowl, mix together tamari, sweet soy sauce or brown sugar, cornstarch, and water. Blend until there are no lumps. Set aside.

Heat large pan or wok over medium-high heat. Add sesame oil and heat for 15 seconds. Add garlic to hot oil and sauté for about 30 seconds. Add broccoli, stirring to coat pieces with oil and garlic. Add mushrooms, if using. Cover and let cook for 2 to 3 minutes, adding a little water, if necessary, to keep broccoli from sticking. Add tamari-cornstarch mixture and stir until thickened, about 30 seconds. Serve over rice and sprinkle with black pepper and sesame seeds. Serves 4.

Note: Sweet soy sauce is a syrupy variety of soy sauce available in Asian food stores.

CURRIED CARROT-SQUASH SOUP

If you want to wow your family (or a special someone) with an elegant meal, serve up some of this soup with a crusty bread and salad. It's so easy to make, but it also proves that vegetarian food is far from boring. (If you can find fresh rosemary and thyme, use them instead of the dried kind for extra flavor.)

2 cups chopped carrots

3 cups peeled, cubed squash

4 cups water

1 cup vegetable broth

1 large leek or 2 green onions, sliced

2 cloves garlic, pressed

½ tsp. rosemary

½ tsp. thyme

½ tsp. tarragon (optional)

½ tsp. salt

½ tsp. pepper

1 tsp. curry powder

1 cup soymilk or dairy milk

1 tsp. lemon juice or vinegar

In a large soup pot, cook carrots and squash in water until soft. In a skillet, heat vegetable broth and add leek or onions, garlic, herbs, salt, pepper, and curry powder. Sauté for 3 minutes, or until leek or onions are tender. Remove from heat and add to carrot-squash mixture.

In blender or food processor, spoon or pour as much of carrot-squash-leek mixture as will fit. Blend on high until smooth, about 30 seconds. Continue until all soup is blended.

Return mixture to soup pot and add soymilk or dairy milk and lemon juice or vinegar. Stir over medium-low heat until warmed through. Serves 6.

BUILD-YOUR-OWN BURRITO

What's more fun than a meal where people pitch in to assemble their own creations? This recipe might look like it has a lot of steps, but each part is really easy. (You don't have to make both the beans *and* the textured vegetable protein filling; they're listed here for variety and to get you experimenting.) Cooking the rice in broth makes it more flavorful, but you could just cook it in water.

Tasty rice:

1 cup rice (brown or white)

2 cups vegetable broth

½ tsp. hot sauce

¼ tsp. chili powder or cumin (optional)

Salt to taste

In medium saucepan, bring rice and broth to boil. Reduce heat, cover, and cook until rice is done (about 15 minutes for white rice, 45 minutes for brown). Add seasonings and set aside.

Bean filling:

½ cup bean cooking liquid (from can or from cooking your own beans)

1 to 3 cloves garlic, minced

½ cup chopped onion

3 cups cooked black beans or pinto beans (you can use
canned or cook your own from dried)
Salt and pepper to taste
Hot sauce to taste

In a large skillet over medium heat, sauté onion and garlic
in bean cooking liquid for 2 minutes. Add beans and seasonings and heat several minutes, until thoroughly warmed.

Fakey meat filling:

1 cup textured vegetable protein (TVP ®) chunks or
    granules
⅞ cup boiling water
¼ cup finely chopped onion
¼ cup finely chopped green pepper
1 tsp. chili powder
½ tsp. cumin (optional)
½ tsp. salt
½ tsp. pepper
Water

Add textured vegetable protein chunks to water, cover, and
soak for 10 minutes (turn off heat; do not cook). Add remaining ingredients, stir, and cook for about 4 or 5 minutes, adding
enough water to keep moist.

Salsa filling:

1½ cups chopped tomato
½ cup chopped onion
2 Tbs. chopped cilantro

Other burrito toppings:

Chopped or shredded lettuce

Chopped avocado (or guacamole)

Chopped zucchini

Chopped mushrooms

Shredded soy cheese or dairy cheese

Soy sour cream or dairy sour cream

Burrito wrappings:

Plenty of large flour tortillas (see note)

To assemble: Set tortilla on a large plate. Scoop some rice onto the tortilla and then some beans and/or fakey meat filling. Top with salsa, veggies, cheese, or other fillings. (Don't overfill or it will be too hard to eat.) Wrap tortilla snugly around ingredients. Eat with your hands, or with a knife and fork. Makes 8 or so burritos.

Note about tortillas: To soften up tortillas before wrapping, steam them over a little water in a large pot fitted with a steamer basket, or warm them in a toaster oven for about 30 seconds.

PASTA WITH TOMATOES AND VEGGIES

Sonnet likes to use okra in this dish, but you can use whatever vegetable you like best. It's especially good with dark leafy greens like chopped kale or spinach.

2 tsp. olive oil

2 Tbs. fresh pressed garlic (4 to 6 cloves)

½ cup chopped onion

4 cups chopped or sliced vegetable (such as okra, kale, spinach, green beans, or zucchini)

4 cups chopped tomatoes (or a 28-ounce can of chopped
     or puréed tomatoes)
½ cup fresh chopped basil leaves (packed)
2 Tbs. tamari or soy sauce
Salt and pepper
6 cups cooked pasta (fettucine, *radiatore,* or spiral-shaped)
Nutritional yeast (optional)
Grated soy cheese or dairy cheese (optional)

In heavy saucepan, sauté onion and garlic in oil for 1 minute,
stirring often. Add vegetable and one cup of the fresh tomatoes.
(If using canned tomatoes, you can add the whole can at this
time.) Cover and cook for 8 minutes over medium-low heat,
stirring occasionally. Add basil and remaining tomatoes (if
using fresh) and heat over high heat until just hot. Stir in tamari
or soy sauce and salt and pepper to taste. Combine vegetable
mixture with pasta, reheat if necessary, and serve. If desired,
sprinkle with nutritional yeast (use as you would Parmesan
cheese) or grated soy cheese or dairy cheese. Serves 4 to 6.

OVEN-BAKED FRENCH FRIES

If you're a fry fanatic, try these lower-fat versions for a side
dish or a snack.

4 to 5 large baking potatoes
1 Tbs. oil
Salt to taste

Heat oven to 400°. Peel potatoes and cut into french
fry–shaped strips about ½ inch wide. Place in a single layer on

a large cookie sheet. Drizzle potatoes with oil, using hands to coat evenly. Bake under oven broiler for 10 minutes, or until potatoes are golden on top. Remove the sheet of potatoes from broiler, place on bottom shelf of oven, and continue baking for 20 more minutes, or until potatoes are tender. Salt to taste, and serve with ketchup. Serves 6.

LUNCH-BOX CREATIONS

You can scoop any of these fillings into pita bread for an easy-to-transport sandwich. (They also make great dips for parties.)

NO-EGG EGG SALAD

1 package firm tofu, drained and crumbled

¼ cup finely chopped carrot

2 Tbs. finely chopped green or red bell pepper

¼ cup finely chopped celery (optional)

2 Tbs. finely chopped green onion

1 tsp. turmeric

½ tsp. salt

½ tsp. black pepper

½ to 1 tsp. hot sauce

1 to 2 tsp. vinegar

1 tsp. mustard

1 Tbs. soy mayonnaise (optional)

Mix together ingredients. Serves 6 to 8.

BABA GANOUJ (TANGY EGGPLANT DIP)

2 medium eggplants

3 Tbs. tahini

2 cloves garlic, pressed

Juice of 1 lemon

2 Tbs. chopped fresh parsley (optional)

½ tsp. salt

Black pepper to taste

Heat oven to 300°. Pierce eggplants with a fork and bake whole until eggplants begin to deflate (about 40 minutes). Let cool completely, scoop out insides, and mash with a fork. Add remaining ingredients and mix well. Serves 6 to 8.

HUMMUS (ZESTY CHICKPEA DIP)

1 can chickpeas, drained (or 1 ½ cups cooked from dried
    beans)

1 to 2 cloves garlic, pressed

Juice of 1 lemon

1 green onion, finely chopped

1 Tbs. chopped fresh parsley

1 to 2 Tbs. tahini

Salt or tamari to taste

Black pepper to taste

Blend all ingredients together in a food processor or blender (or mash really well in a bowl). Serves 4.

PESTO PASTA SALAD

Pesto is usually made with Parmesan cheese, but this vegan version has more than enough pizzazz without it. Pack in an airtight container for a sensational, savory lunch.

½ cup water

1 Tbs. arrowroot or cornstarch

1 cup packed fresh basil leaves

1 to 2 Tbs. fresh pressed garlic

½ tsp. salt (or to taste)

1 Tbs. nutritional yeast

1 Tbs. tamari or soy sauce

6 cups cooked pasta spirals (or other favorite pasta shape)

3 cups chopped tomatoes

½ cup sliced black olives (optional)

½ cup green peas, thawed from frozen (optional)

In large bowl, mix together cooked pasta and tomatoes. Set aside.

In a small saucepan over high heat, whisk together water and arrowroot or cornstarch until thickened. In blender, combine water-arrowroot or -cornstarch mixture, basil leaves, garlic, salt, nutritional yeast, and tamari or soy sauce. Blend well. Pour sauce over pasta and tomatoes and stir well. Add olives and green peas if using. Serves 8.

SWEET TREATS

BANANA-OAT MUFFINS

It's not so hard to bake without eggs, as these tasty muffins show. Enjoy them with yogurt or jam for breakfast.

Topping:

    1 tsp. cinnamon

    ½ cup brown sugar, lightly packed

    1 Tbs. margarine or oil

    ¾ cup rolled oats

Muffins:

    1½ cups whole-wheat pastry flour (see note)

    1 cup unbleached white flour

    1 tsp. nutmeg

    ¼ cup chopped walnuts (optional)

    1 tsp. baking powder

    1½ tsp. baking soda

    ¼ tsp. salt

    ½ cup liquid sweetener (such as honey or maple syrup)

    1 cup mashed, very ripe banana (about 2 medium-large
        bananas)

    2 Tbs. oil

    1 tsp. vanilla

    ¼ tsp. lemon extract

    Water

Stir together topping ingredients and set aside.

Heat oven to 350°. In a bowl, mix together flours, nutmeg, walnuts (if using), baking powder, baking soda, and salt. In a separate bowl, mix together liquid sweetener, bananas, oil, vanilla, lemon extract, and enough water to make 2 ¼ cups of liquid (about ⅝ cup of water). Mix together wet and dry mixtures just until blended and spoon into lightly oiled or nonstick muffin pans. Sprinkle with topping and bake until muffin tops spring back when lightly touched, about 25 minutes. Makes 10 to 12 muffins.

Note: You can use all unbleached white flour, if desired (a total of 2½ cups).

APPLE CRISP

This dessert is as tasty as apple pie but easier to make and better for you, too. Great topped with ice cream (either the dairy or the nondairy kind).

Filling:
   8 cups cored, peeled, and sliced apples
   2 tsp. cinnamon
   ½ tsp. nutmeg
   1 Tbs. arrowroot powder or cornstarch
   Juice of ½ lemon
   2 Tbs. honey or maple syrup
   ¼ cup apple juice (use if apples don't seem very juicy)

Topping:
   ⅔ cup barley flour or whole-wheat flour
   ¼ cup whole-wheat flour
   ⅓ cup brown sugar, lightly packed
   ¼ cup chopped walnuts
   ⅓ cup rolled oats
   ½ tsp. cinnamon
   ½ tsp. nutmeg

¼ tsp. salt

Juice of ½ lemon

2 Tbs. honey or maple syrup

1 Tbs. oil

Heat oven to 350°.

Filling: In a large bowl, mix together all filling ingredients. Put apple mixture into a 9" pie plate.

Topping: In a medium-sized bowl, combine flour(s) and next 6 ingredients. Stir lemon juice, honey or maple syrup, and oil into dry mixture and blend well (it will be necessary to use your hands to mix it). Sprinkle topping over filling and bake until topping is browned and apples are soft, about 30 minutes. Serves 8.

CHOCOLATE SNACKING CAKE

When your sweet tooth craves chocolate, whip up this simple snack. No eggs, no dairy, and a lot less fat than most chocolate cakes.

½ cup cocoa or carob powder

1½ tsp. baking powder

1 tsp. baking soda

1 ⅓ cups unbleached white flour or whole-wheat pastry
    flour, or combination of both

½ cup brown sugar, lightly packed

¼ cup white sugar

¼ tsp. salt

1¼ cup coffee (regular or decaffeinated; brewed or made
    from instant)

¼ cup applesauce

1½ Tbs. oil

¼ cup honey or maple syrup

2 tsp. vanilla

¼ tsp. lemon extract (or orange, rum, or maple extract)

2 Tbs. dark (semisweet) chocolate chips or carob chips
(see note)

2 Tbs. slivered almonds or chopped walnuts

Heat oven to 325˚. Sift together cocoa, baking powder, and baking soda and stir into flour. Mix in sugars and salt. In a separate bowl, mix together coffee, applesauce, oil, honey or maple syrup, vanilla, and lemon extract. Pour wet ingredients into flour mixture and beat thoroughly. Stir in chocolate chips. Pour batter into a lightly oiled and floured 9 x 9" pan (or 9" round pan) and sprinkle with nuts. Bake for 40 minutes or until toothpick inserted in center comes out clean. Serves 8 to 10.

Note about chocolate chips: Some dark chocolate chips contain dairy products; many don't. If you want to make a completely dairy-free cake, read ingredient listings and choose dairy-free chips.

Variation #1: Instead of mixing the chocolate or carob chips into the cake, sprinkle them on top before baking, along with the nuts.

Variation #2: To make cupcakes, spoon batter into muffin tins lined with foil or paper cupcake liners. Sprinkle top with nuts, and reduce baking time to about 30 minutes.

APPENDICES

APPENDIX 1

RESOURCES

FOR FURTHER READING

Beyond Beef by Jeremy Rifkin. New York: Dutton, 1992.

Diet for a New America by John Robbins. Walpole, New Hampshire: Stillpoint Publishing, 1987.

Diet for a Small Planet, 20th Anniversary Edition, by Frances Moore Lappé. New York: Ballantine Books, 1991.

For the Vegetarian in You by Billy Ray Boyd. Santa Cruz, CA: Taterhill, 1987.

The Healthy School Action Guide by Susan Campbell and Todd Winant. Santa Cruz, CA: EarthSave Foundation, 1994.

The Jungle by Upton Sinclair. Many editions available.

May All Be Fed by John Robbins. New York: William Morrow, 1992.

Vegan Nutrition: Pure and Simple by Michael Klaper, M.D. Umatilla, FL: Gentle World, 1987.

Vegetarian Journal's Guide to Natural Foods Restaurants from the Vegetarian Resource Group. Garden City Park, NY: Avery Publishing Group, 1993.

COOKBOOKS

The Compassionate Cook by People for the Ethical Treatment of Animals and Ingrid Newkirk. New York: Warner Books, 1993. Easy, fun-to-make, totally animal-free fare.

The Moosewood Cookbook, 15th Anniversary Edition, by Mollie Katzen. Berkeley, CA: Ten Speed Press, 1992. An updated version of an old vegetarian standby.

The Natural Gourmet by Annemarie Colbin. New York: Ballentine Books, 1989. Uncomplicated but elegant recipes.

The New Farm Vegetarian Cookbook edited by Louise Hagler and Dorothy R. Bates. Summertown, TN: Book Publishing Company, 1988. Lots of hearty, easy recipes.

The New Laurel's Kitchen by Laurel Robertson, Brian Ruppenthal, and Carol Flinders. Berkeley, CA: Ten Speed Press, 1993. A classic for vegetarian cooks.

New Recipes for Young Vegetarians by Sammy Green. London: Foulsham, 1988. (Distributed in the United States by Atrium, Lower Lake, CA.) Health information and easy-to-make recipes.

New Vegetarian Cuisine by Linda Rosensweig and food editors of *Prevention* magazine. Emmaus, PA: Rodale Press, 1994. Hip recipes, plus info on veggie nutrition.

Nikki & David Goldbeck's American Wholefoods Cuisine by Nikki and David Goldbeck. New York: Plume/NAL, 1983. More than 1,300 great-tasting, easy-to-understand recipes.

The Savory Way by Deborah Madison. New York: Bantam, 1990. When you're ready for more sophisticated cuisine and somewhat more complex recipes.

Simply Vegan: Quick Vegetarian Meals by Debra Wasserman and Reed Mangels, Ph.D., R.D. Baltimore, MD: Vegetarian Resource Group, 1991. The name says it all.

Still Life with Menu by Mollie Katzen. Berkeley, CA: Ten Speed Press, 1988. Delicious recipes; beautiful illustrations.

The Vegetarian Lunchbasket by Linda Haynes. Willow Springs, MO: Nucleus Publishing, 1990. Two hundred and twenty-five brown-bag lunch ideas.

PERIODICALS

Ahimsa, 501 Old Harding Highway, Malaga, NJ 08328. Quarterly magazine of the American Vegan Society. Addresses ethical issues.

How On Earth!, P.O. Box 3347, West Chester, PA 19381. The ultimate news source for vegetarian teens and others who support "compassionate, ecologically sound living." Written by teenagers.

Natural Health, 17 Station Street, Brookline Village, MA 02147. Includes information about nutrition, natural foods, and alternative medicine.

Otterwise, P.O. Box 1374, Portland, ME 04104. For kids who are into saving animals and the environment.

Vegetarian Gourmet, P.O. Box 7641, Riverton, NJ 08077-7641. A magazine full of meatless recipes.

Vegetarian Journal, P.O. Box 1463, Baltimore, MD 21203. Magazine of the Vegetarian Resource Group.

Vegetarian Times, P.O. Box 570, Oak Park, IL 60303. Articles covering everything from how to cook with tofu to tips for vegetarian travelers. Stories on health and the environment and plenty of new recipes every month.

Vegetarian Voice, P.O. Box 72, Dolgeville, NY 13329. Magazine of the North American Vegetarian Society.

Veggie Life, 1401 Shary Circle, Concord, CA 95418. Information about vegetarian eating and organic gardening.

VEGETARIAN GROUPS

These national organizations provide excellent support for the new vegetarian. You can order books from them, get recipe ideas, and learn where to find other vegetarians in your area.

American Vegan Society, 501 Old Harding Highway, Malaga, NJ 08328; (609) 694-2887. Promotes a diet free of all animal products.

North American Vegetarian Society, P.O. Box 72, Dolgeville, NY 13329; (518) 568-7970. This is the group that put World Vegetarian Day on the calendar (October 1). Distributes a booklet discussing the most commonly asked questions about vegetarianism. Special student membership rate.

Vegetarian Education Network (VE-Net), P.O. Box 3347, West Chester, PA 19381; (717) 529-8638. Supports young vegetarians and promotes the teaching of vegetarian issues in schools. Publishes *How On Earth!*.

Vegetarian Resource Group, P.O. Box 1463, Baltimore, MD 21203; (410) 366-VEGE. Send a self-addressed, stamped envelope for info, including a brochure on nutrition for teenagers. Special student membership rate.

ENVIRONMENTAL GROUPS

EarthSave Foundation, P.O. Box 68, Santa Cruz, CA 95063-0068; (408) 423-4069. The only big environmental organization with a strong vegetarian perspective.

Ranching Task Force, P.O. Box 5784, Tucson, AZ 85703; (602) 578-3173. Provides information on the hazards of western grazing.

The YES! (Youth for Environmental Sanity) Tour, 706 Frederick St., Santa Cruz, CA 95062; (408) 459-9344. Teen-organized speaking tour.

ANIMAL-RIGHTS FOLKS

Animalearn, a project of the American Anti-Vivisection Society, 801 Old York Road, #204, Jenkintown, PA 19046-1685; (215) 887-0816. Animal-rights info especially for students. Holds summer programs and workshops.

Dissection Hotline, a project of the North American Vegetarian Society; (609) 694-2887. Provides advice and information to students seeking alternatives to animal dissection.

Farm Animal Reform Movement (FARM), 10101 Ashburton Lane, Bethesda, MD 20817; (301) 530-1737. Factory farm information.

Farm Sanctuary, P.O. Box 150, Watkins Glen, NY 14891; (607) 583-2225. Provides a home to rescued farm animals. Offers an internship for teenagers at both its New York and California locations.

People for the Ethical Treatment of Animals (PETA), P.O. Box 42516, Washington, DC 20015-0516; (301) 770-PETA. Has a vegetarian campaign and a program for kids.

HEALTH AND NUTRITION ORGANIZATIONS

Center for Science in the Public Interest, 1875 Connecticut Ave. NW, Suite 300, Washington, DC 20009-5728; (202) 332-9110. Publishes *Nutrition Action Newsletter* and runs a youth campaign called Kids Against Junk Food.

Physicians Committee for Responsible Medicine, P.O. Box 6322, Washington, DC 20015; (202) 686-2210. Publishes *Good Medicine*, including informative articles on health and nutrition.

The Vegetarian Nutrition Dietetic Practice Group (a subgroup of the American Dietetic Association), 216 W. Jackson Blvd., Chicago, IL 60606. Nutrition hotline: (800) 366-1655.

FOR INFO ON A VEGETARIAN DIET IN WORLD RELIGIONS

Interfaith Council for the Protection of Animals and Nature, 4290 Raintree Lane NW, Atlanta, GA 30327; (404) 252-9176.

International Network for Religion and Animals, P.O. Box 1335, North Wales, PA 19454-0335; (215) 721-1908. Publishes *INRoAds* magazine.

OTHER GOOD PEOPLE TO KNOW ABOUT

Beyond Beef, 1130 Seventeenth St. NW, Suite 300, Washington, DC 20036. Teaches people about the health, environmental, and ethical costs of eating meat. Many teens have participated in its Adopt-a-McDonald's campaign to inform the public about the facts of meat production.

The Healthy School Lunch Program (a project of EarthSave Foundation), 706 Frederick St., Santa Cruz, CA 95062; (408) 423-4069. Information about getting vegetarian food served in your school cafeteria, including a comprehensive action handbook for students, parents, and teachers.

CONTESTS AND AWARDS

Annual Vegetarian Essay Contest, sponsored by the Vegetarian Resource Group, P.O. Box 1463, Baltimore, MD 21203. To enter, you write a two- to three-page essay on any vegetarian issue and postmark it by May 1 of the year. Three winners are selected from these age categories: 14 to 18; 9 to 13; and 8 and under. Winners receive a savings bond. Include name, age, grade, school, and name of your teacher. (You don't have to be vegetarian to enter.)

Bill Rosenberg Award, sponsored by the Farm Animal Reform Movement, 10101 Ashburton Lane, Bethesda, MD 20817. Annually awarded to a person age 18 or under who has made a substantial difference in ending farm-animal abuse. Send a one-page statement about you or the person you're nominating by September 24 of the year. Money awarded.

Student Animal Advocate Award, sponsored by Animalearn, a branch of the American Anti-Vivisection Society, 801 Old York Road, #204, Jenkintown, PA 19046. Awarded to two secondary school students working on behalf of animals. If you nominate yourself, you need a letter of recommendation. Money awarded. Contact Animalearn for an application.

Young Activist Campaign Contest, sponsored by the American Anti-Vivisection Society (see address above). Encourages young people to work together to develop fun and effective campaigns against animal suffering and other societal problems. Open to groups of people from elementary school through college. Money awarded. Deadline for applications is April 15 of each year. Contact the American Anti-Vivisection Society for application.

MAIL-ORDER VEGETARIAN FOOD

If you'd like to try some new vegetarian foods but don't have a lot to choose from at your local stores, don't worry. You can purchase everything by mail—from vegetarian instant lunches to cruelty-free bath products. Here are some companies you can contact for catalogs.

Clear Eye Natural Foods, 302 Rte. 89 South, Savannah, NY 13146; (800) 724-2233.

Garden Spot Distributors, 438 White Oak Road, New Holland, PA 17557; (800) 829-5100.

Good Eats, P.O. Box 756, Richboro, PA 18954; (215) 364-8069.

Heartland Foods, R.R. 2, Box 189 B, Susquehanna, PA 18847; (717) 879-8790.

Jaffe Bros., P.O. Box 636, Valley Center, CA 92082-0636; (619) 749-1133.

Mail Order Catalog, P.O. Box 180, Summertown, TN 38483; (800) 695-2241.

Shiloh Farms, 1 Hibler St., Sulphur Springs, AR 72768; (215) 362-6832.

Walnut Acres, Penns Creek, PA 17862; (717) 837-0601.

APPENDIX 2

REFERENCES

INTRODUCTION

Arnold, Andrea. "Confessions of a Teenage Vegetarian," *Conscious Choice*, September/October 1993, p. 24.

Bittman, Mark. "I Was a Teen-Age Vegetarian," *The New York Times Magazine*, October 3, 1993, p. 63.

Brink, Susan. "So Long, Big Macs—It's On to Rice and Beans," *U.S. News & World Report*, May 10, 1993, pp. 70–71.

Mathias, Barbara. "Pass the Meat: The Growth of Vegetarian Teens," *The Washington Post*, August 25, 1992.

Krizmanic, Judy. "Here's Who We Are," *Vegetarian Times*, October 1992, pp. 72–80.

Pappano, Laura. "Teens Who Go Green," *The Boston Globe*, September 30, 1992, Food section.

CHAPTER I
WHAT IS A VEGETARIAN, ANYWAY?

Human Rights and Hunger Issues
Lappé, Frances Moore, and Collins, Joseph. *Food First: Beyond the Myth of Scarcity.* Boston: Houghton Mifflin, 1977.

Ethics

Moran, Victoria. *Compassion, The Ultimate Ethic: An Exploration of Veganism.* Wellingborough, Northamptonshire, Great Britain: Thorsons, 1985.

Religious Reasons

Regenstein, Lewis G. *Replenish the Earth.* New York: Crossroad Publishing Company, 1991.

Feminism

Wiley, Carol. "The Feminist Connection," *Vegetarian Times,* January 1991, pp. 59–65, 80.

Celebrities

Fishman, Laurel. "They're Glitz, Glam and Veg," *Vegetarian Times,* February 1994, pp. 60–63.

CHAPTER 2
FOR THE PLANET

General

Durning, Alan, and Brough, Holly. *Taking Stock: Animal Farming and the Environment,* Worldwatch Paper No. 103. Washington, DC: Worldwatch Institute, July 1991.

Durning, Alan. "Cost of Beef for Health and Habitat," *Los Angeles Times,* Sept. 21, 1986.

EarthSave Foundation. *Our Food Our World: The Realities of an Animal-Based Diet.* Santa Cruz, CA: EarthSave, 1992.

Fletcher, Susan. "Tropical Deforestation: International Implications." Reprinted in *Global Environment,* 102nd Congress, 2nd Session, Senate Document No. 102–13. National debate topic for high schools, 1992–1993.

Pimentel, David. *Food, Energy and the Future of Society.* Boulder: Colorado Associated University Press, 1980.

Pimentel, David and Marcia. *Food, Energy and Society.* London: Edward Arnold Ltd., 1979.

Postel, Sandra. *Last Oasis: Facing Water Scarcity.* New York: Norton/Worldwatch Institute, 1992.

USDA Economic Research Service.

United States Bureau of Land Management and United States Forest Service (Range Management).

Public Lands Ranching

Jacobs, Lynn. *Waste of the West: Public Lands Ranching.* Tucson, AZ: Jacobs, 1991.

Wuerthner, George. "The Price Is Wrong," *Sierra*, September/October 1990, pp. 38–43.

Fish

Krizmanic, Judy. "Getting Unhooked," *Vegetarian Times*, March 1990, pp. 43–50.

Duff, Fergus. "Vegetarianism and the Environment," *Vegetarian Issues: A Resource Pack for Secondary Schools.* England: The Vegetarian Society of the United Kingdom, 1992.

CHAPTER 3
FOR THE ANIMALS

Mason, Jim, and Singer, Peter. *Animal Factories.* New York: Harmony Books, 1990.

Singer, Peter. *Animal Liberation.* New York: New York Review of Books, 1990.

Weil, Zoe. *Animals in Society: Facts and Perspectives on Our Treatment of Animals.* Jenkintown, PA: Animalearn (The American Anti-Vivisection Society), 1991.

CHAPTER 4
FOR YOUR HEALTH

Veg Diet OK for Teens

Havala, S., M.S., R.D., and Dwyer, J., D.Sc., R.D. "Position of the American Dietetic Association: Vegetarian Diets," *Journal of the American Dietetic Association.* 1993; 93: 1317–19.

Havala, S., M.S., R.D., and Dwyer, J., D.Sc., R.D. "Position of the American Dietetic Association: Vegetarian Diets," *Journal of the American Dietetic Association.* 1988; 88: 351–55.

Veg Teens Grow Just Fine

Mangels, A. R. "Vegetarian Infants and Children: A Review of Recent Research," *Issues in Vegetarian Dietetics*, Winter 1991; Vol. I, No. 2: 4–6.

O'Connell, J.M., M.H.S., et al. "Growth of Vegetarian Children: The Farm Study," *Pediatrics*, 1989; 84 (3): 475–81.

Veg Teens in Line with Dietary Recommendations

Johnston, P. K. "The Vegetarian Adolescent," *Adolescent Medicine: State of the Art Reviews*, October 1992; Vol. 3, No. 3: 417–37.

Mountains of Evidence for a Vegetarian Diet

First International Congress on Vegetarian Nutrition, *The American Journal of Clinical Nutrition* (Suppl.), 1988; 48: 707–927.

Horgan, Karin. "Vegetarianism Bolstered," *Vegetarian Times,* October 1992, p. 18.

Heart Disease

Snowdon, D. A., Phillips, R. L., and Fraser, G. E. "Meat Consumption and Fatal Ischemic Heart Disease," *Preventive Medicine,* 1984; 13: 490–500.

Burr, M. L., and Butland, B. K. "Heart Disease in British Vegetarians," *American Journal of Clinical Nutrition* (Suppl.), 1988; 48: 830–32.

Ornish, Dean, M.D. *Dr. Dean Ornish's Program for Reversing Heart Disease.* New York: Random House, 1990.

Knuiman, J. T., and West, C. E. "The Concentration of Cholesterol in Serum and in Various Serum Lipoproteins in Macrobiotic, Vegetarian and Nonvegetarian Men and Boys," *Atherosclerosis,* 1982; 43: 71–82.

Pelkie, Chuck. "Heart-Stopping Findings," *Vegetarian Times,* December 1992, p. 16.

Cancer

Phillips, R. L. "Role of Life-style and Dietary Habits in Risk of Cancer Among Seventh-Day Adventists," *Cancer Research* (Suppl.), 1975; 35: 3513–22.

Dwyer, J. T. "Health Aspects of Vegetarianism," *American Journal of Clinical Nutrition* (Suppl.), 1988; 48: 712–38.

Barnard, Neal, M.D. "The Edge Against Cancer," *Vegetarian Times,* October 1991, pp. 18–21.

Other Illness

Dwyer, J. T. "Health Aspects of Vegetarianism," *American Journal of Clinical Nutrition* (Suppl.), 1988; 48: 712–38.

Snowdon, D. A., et. al. "Does a Vegetarian Diet Reduce the Occurence of Diabetes?" *American Journal of Public Health*, 1985; 75: 507–12.

Pixley, F., et. al. "Effect of Vegetarianism on Development of Gallstones in Women," *British Medical Journal*, 1985: 291.

Marsh, A.G., et al. "Vegetarian Lifestyle and Bone Mineral Density," *American Journal of Clinical Nutrition* (Suppl.), 1988; 48: 837–41.

Abelow, B., et. al. "Cross Cultural Association Between Dietary Animal Protein and Hip Fracture: A Hypothesis," *Calcified Tissue International*, 1992; 50: 14–18.

Krizmanic, Judy. "Calcium Competition," *Vegetarian Times*, February 1994, p. 16.

Fatigue

Messina, Virginia, M.P.H., R.D. "Ask Ginny," *How On Earth!*, Spring 1993, p. 3.

Lark, Susan, M.D. "The Low-Energy Blues," *Vegetarian Times*, February 1992, p. 18.

Weight

Ornish, Dean, M.D. *Eat More, Weigh Less: Dr. Dean Ornish's Life Choice Program for Losing Weight While Eating Abundantly.* New York: HarperCollins, 1993.

Athletics

Krizmanic, Judy. "Facts for Fueling Up," *Vegetarian Times*, August 1990, pp. 51–54, 71.

PMS

Lark, Susan, M.D. *Menstrual Cramps: A Self-Help Program.* Los Altos, CA: Westchester Publishing Co., 1993.

Horrobin, D. F. "The Role of Essential Fatty Acids and Prostaglandins in the Premenstrual Syndrome," *Journal of Reproductive Medicine*, 1983; 28(7): 465.

Hirayama, T. Paper presented at Conference on Breast Cancer and Diet, U.S.–Japan Cooperative Cancer Research Program, Fred Hutchison Cancer Center, Seattle, WA, March 14–15, 1977, as cited in Robbins, John, *Diet for a New America*, Walpole, NH: Stillpoint Publishing, 1987.

Acne

Lark, Susan, M.D. "The Skinny on Teen Skin," *Vegetarian Times*, March 1993, pp. 104–05.

Pizzorno, Joseph E., Jr., N.D. "Facing Up to Acne," *Vegetarian Times*, January 1992, pp. 18–19.

Protein

Johnston, P. K. "The Vegetarian Adolescent," *Adolescent Medicine: State of the Art Reviews*, October 1992; Vol. 3, No. 3: 417–37.

Iron

Johnston, P. K. "The Vegetarian Adolescent," *Adolescent Medicine: State of the Art Reviews*, October 1992; Vol. 3, No. 3: 417–37.

Krizmanic, Judy. "Desperately Seeking Iron," *Vegetarian Times*, March 1992, pp. 66–72.

Calcium

Heaney, Robert P., M.D., John A. Creighton University Professor, Creighton University, Omaha, NE. Personal communication with author, November 1993.

Messina, Virginia, M.P.H., R.D., Mount Airy, MD. Personal communication with author, February 1993.

Weaver, C., and Plawecki, K. "Dietary Calcium: Adequacy of a Vegetarian Diet," *American Journal of Clinical Nutrition*, 1994: 59 (in press).

Vitamin B_{12}

Messina, Virginia, M.P.H., R.D. "Ask Ginny," *How On Earth!*, Spring 1993, p. 3.

Klaper, Michael, M.D., Director, Institute of Nutrition Education and Research, Manhattan Beach, CA. Personal communication with author, June 1993.

Cullen, Sally H. "B_{12} or Not B_{12}?" *Vegetarian Times*, December 1992, pp. 57–61.

Chicken and Fish

Puzo, Daniel P. "Meat Inspection 'No Longer Adequate,' " *Los Angeles Times*, February 11, 1993.

Editors of *Consumer Reports*. "Is Our Fish Fit to Eat?", *Consumer Reports*, February 1992, pp. 103–20.

Hold the Bacteria

Center for Science in the Public Interest. *Safe Food: Eating Wisely in a Risky World*. Los Angeles: Living Planet, 1991.

CHAPTER 5
MAKING THE SWITCH

Amato, Paul, Ph.D., and Partridge, Sonia A. *The New Vegetarians: Promoting Health and Protecting Life*. New York: Plenum Press, 1989.

Hoemeke, Laura. "It's Your Move," *Vegetarian Times*, June 1988, pp. 40–46.

Krizmanic, Judy. "I Really Want To But . . ." *Vegetarian Times*, January 1992, pp. 34–40.

CHAPTER 6
WHAT WILL YOUR PARENTS SAY?

General

Dunn, Douglas. "You're Going To Be a What?!" *Vegetarian Times*, November 1991, pp. 60–63.

Ringer, Jill. "Convince Your Parents!" *How On Earth!*, Summer 1992, p. 8.

Yntema, Sharon. *Vegetarian Children: A Supportive Guide for Parents*. Ithaca, NY: McBooks Press, 1987.

Tradition

Atlas, Nava. *Vegetarian Celebrations: Menus for Holidays and Other Festive Occasions*. Boston: Little, Brown & Co., 1990.

CHAPTER 7
WHAT WILL YOUR FRIENDS SAY?

Wiley, Carol. "Vegetarian Mythconceptions: Perception vs. Reality," *Vegetarian Times*, March 1990, pp. 36–41.

CHAPTER 8
STICKY SITUATIONS

Fast Food

"Vegetarian Express: Fast Food Campaign," a brochure of the North American Vegetarian Society, Dolgeville, NY.

Peters, Loretta. "Vegetarian Travelers vs. Fast Food," *Vegetarian Times*, September 1991, pp. 73–77.

Travel

Krizmanic, Judy. "An American Veg in Paris," *Vegetarian Times*, May 1993, pp. 28–30.

CHAPTER 9
SURVIVING AT SCHOOL

School Lunch

Campbell, Susan, and Winant, Todd. *The Healthy School Lunch Action Guide*. Santa Cruz, CA: EarthSave Foundation, 1994.

Dissection

Francione, Gary L., and Charlton, Anna E. *Vivisection and Dissection in the Classroom: A Guide to Conscientious Objection*. Jenkintown, PA: The American Anti-Vivisection Society, 1992.

Shoesmith Stephens, Jo. "Dissection," *Animal Guardian*, Vol. 5., No. 4, 1992.

CHAPTER 10
SOME NUTRITION BASICS

General

The Vegetarian Nutrition Dietetic Practice Group of the American Dietetic Association. *Issues in Vegetarian Dietetics*, Vol. I, No. 1–Vol. II, No. 1.

First International Congress on Vegetarian Nutrition, *The American Journal of Clinical Nutrition* (Suppl.), 1988; 48: 707–927.

Gershoff, Stanley, Ph.D., ed. *The Tufts University Guide to Total Nutrition*. New York: Harper & Row, 1990.

Johnston, P. K. "The Vegetarian Adolescent," *Adolescent Medicine: State of the Art Reviews*, October 1992; Vol. 3, No. 3: 417–37.

Messina, Virginia, M.P.H., R.D. Nutrition section of the *Vegetarian Curriculum and Activities Guide for Teachers*. West Chester, PA: Vegetarian Education Network, 1994.

Nutrient Contents of Foods

Pennington, Jean A.T. *Food Values of Portions Commonly Used*. New York: HarperCollins, 1989.

Wasserman, Debra, and Mangels, Reed, Ph.D., R.D. *Simply Vegan*. Baltimore, MD: Vegetarian Resource Group, 1991.

Eating Disorder

Krizmanic, Judy. "Perfection Obsession: Can Vegetarianism Cover Up an Eating Disorder?" *Vegetarian Times*, June 1992, pp. 54–60.

CHAPTER 11
FABULOUS VEGETARIAN FOODS

Bates, Dorothy R. *The TVP® Cookbook.* Summertown, TN: Book Publishing Co., 1991.

Bates, Dorothy R., and Wingate, Colby. *Cooking with Gluten and Seitan.* Summertown, TN: Book Publishing Co., 1993.

Goldbeck, Nikki and David. *The Goldbecks' Guide to Good Food.* New York: NAL Books, 1987.

Hagler, Louise. *Tofu Quick and Easy.* Summertown, TN: Book Publishing Co., 1986.

Obis, Mariclare Barrett. "Take Another Look at Soyfoods," *Vegetarian Times*, August 1993, pp. 54–66.

Shurtleff, William, and Aoyagi, Akiko. *The Book of Tofu.* New York: Ballantine Books, 1979.

CHAPTER 12
THE MAKINGS OF A MEAL

Bates, Dorothy R. *Kids Can Cook.* Summertown, TN: Book Publishing Co., 1987.

Carroll, Mary. "Lunchbox Creations," *Vegetarian Times*, September 1992, pp. 22–27.

Cheney, Susan Jane. "Your Guide to Filling a Veg Pantry," *Vegetarian Times*, July 1993, pp. 72–80.

Haynes, Linda. *The Vegetarian Lunchbasket.* Willow Springs, MO: Nucleus Publications, 1992.

Obis, Mariclare Barrett. "A World of Culinary Opportunity," *Vegetarian Times*, March 1993, pp. 76–81.

Toomay, Mindy, and Geiskopf-Hadler, Susann. *The Best 125 Meatless Main Dishes.* Rocklin, CA: Prima, 1992.

Baking Without Eggs

DeSilver, Drew. "Egg-cellent Substitutes," *Vegetarian Times*, August 1992, pp. 16–18.

Pierce, Sonnet. "Vegetarian Baking!," *How On Earth!*, Spring 1993, p. 7.

Hidden Animal Ingredients

Wiley, Carol. "Why It's Impossible to Be a Vegetarian," *Vegetarian Times*, May 1991, pp. 59–62, 89.

APPENDIX 3

GLOSSARY

Animal agriculture: The farming of animals for meat and other products, such as milk and eggs. Includes the farming of grains to feed such animals.

Animal rights: The belief that all species have the right not to be exploited or killed for human use.

Animal testing: Using animals in safety tests of new products, such as cosmetics and household cleaners.

Aquaculture: The process of raising fish, on fish farms, to be eaten.

Calcium: A mineral that your body needs to build bones and teeth and for maintaining bone strength.

Casein: A milk protein. Added to most soy cheeses and many other "nondairy" products to improve texture. (Sometimes listed as "caseinate" on labels.)

Complex carbohydrates: Nutrients that provide energy and that should make up most of your diet. Found in vegetables, grains, and beans.

Dietitian: A nutrition expert who can help you put together a healthy diet.

Dissection: The process, such as in biology class, of taking apart and analyzing the bodies of animals that have been killed.

Egg replacer: A powdered mix of ingredients that takes the place of eggs in baked goods, such as ENER-G Egg Replacer. Available in natural food stores.

Ethical vegetarian: A person who believes that it is morally wrong to raise animals in an inhumane manner or to kill them for people to eat. Some ethical vegetarians are morally opposed to other aspects of meat production as well, such as feeding grain to livestock animals instead of people, or causing environmental damage through animal agriculture.

Ethnic food: Cuisine from other cultures, including Chinese food, Ethiopian food, Indian food, and Mexican food.

Factory farm: A name for today's high-tech farms where animals are raised.

Fat: A nutrient that is necessary for many body functions, such as supporting cell walls and processing certain vitamins, but unhealthy in large amounts. Too much dietary fat is linked to health problems such as heart disease and certain cancers. Health experts tell us especially to avoid foods high in *saturated* fat (found in meat, dairy products, and coconut and palm oils), as well as *hydrogenated* fats like those in margarines and many processed foods.

Fiber: A type of complex carbohydrate found in plant foods. It helps the body in many ways, such as keeping the intestines healthy and lowering cholesterol levels.

Gelatin: A protein extracted from animal bones, used to stiffen or to gel liquids. It's often added to processed foods, from candies to fat-free yogurt. *Kosher* gelatin is usually vegetarian.

Grain: The seeds and fruits from cereal plants such as rice, corn, wheat, and rye. Grain products include pasta, breads, and crackers.

Iron: A mineral that your body needs for building healthy blood.

Lacto-vegetarian: A diet that omits meat and eggs but includes milk products, or a person who eats this way.

Lard: Animal fat. Often used in refried beans.

Legumes: Another word for beans that grow in pods, such as kidney beans and pinto beans. Includes split peas and lentils. Dried legumes cook up to be hearty and filling.

Livestock production: The process of raising animals for meat.

Macrobiotic: A Japanese diet philosophy that is mostly vegetarian but may include fish.

Miso: A strong-tasting, salty paste made from fermented soybeans, for use as seasoning in soups, stews, salad dressings, bean dishes, and spreads.

Natural food store: A specialty food market that sells many vegetarian products. "Natural foods" generally contain no preservatives or artificial colors and flavors (although not all products with the word "natural" on the label live up to this standard).

Natural hygiene: A lifestyle that promotes the best health possible through fresh air, sunshine, rest, good relationships, and a diet centered around fruits, vegetables, beans, nuts, and seeds.

Ovo-lacto vegetarian: A diet that omits meat but includes eggs and milk products, or a person who eats this way.

Ovo-vegetarian: A diet that omits meat and milk products but includes eggs, or a person who eats this way.

Protein: A nutrient that your body needs for growth, repair, and formation of new tissues.

Rennet: An enzyme from the lining of calves' stomachs, used to make cheese. (Often listed as "enzymes" on labels.)

Seitan (pronounced SAY-tan): A meatlike food made from wheat flour that's been kneaded, boiled, and seasoned. You can make it into sandwiches or use it in main dishes.

Semi-vegetarian: A term that describes someone who has made a partial commitment to vegetarianism. For instance, a semi-vegetarian might eat meat only sometimes (like on holidays). Or a semi-vegetarian might eat some kinds of meat, like fish, all the time, but never other kinds, such as red meat and poultry. (Some people say there's no such thing as a semi-vegetarian; you're vegetarian or you're not.)

Soy cheese: A cheese made from soymilk instead of dairy milk. Comes in many varieties and can be used just like dairy cheese.

Soymilk: A beverage made from soybeans, available in many flavors.

Strict vegetarian: A sort-of-confusing term that can mean a couple of things. Some people use it to mean a person who doesn't eat any animal products at all (see **Total vegetarian**), but some people use it to describe any kind of vegetarian, as long as he or she is pretty serious (for instance, a person who still eats dairy products might be "strict" about not eating meat).

Tahini: A paste made from ground sesame seeds. Use on sandwiches or in dips and sauces.

Tamari: A type of soy sauce.

Tempeh: A food made from cultured soybeans. Comes in dense patties that can be made into sandwiches or used in main dishes.

Textured Vegetable Protein (TVP®): Tiny granules, flakes, or chunks made from soy flour. Turns meatlike when mixed with boiling water.

Tofu: A soyfood that comes in soft white blocks. It soaks up the flavor of many seasonings and can be used in main dishes or desserts.

Total vegetarian: A diet that is completely free of animal products (meat, eggs, dairy products, and honey), or a person who eats this way. Also see **Strict vegetarian**.

Vegan (pronounced VEE-gun): Generally, a diet that omits all animal products, including meat, eggs, dairy products, and honey; or a person who eats this way. The American Vegan Society, however, says that the word *vegan* refers to a whole *lifestyle*, not just diet. According to the AVS, a vegan is someone who does not use animal products for food or clothing (no leather, wool, silk, or goose down), and who strives to avoid animal exploitation in all aspects of his or her life. The AVS suggests that a person who is vegan in diet only should be called a *total vegetarian.*

Vegetarian: A diet that omits meat (beef, pork, poultry, seafood), but that may include other animal products, such as eggs and milk, or a person who eats this way.

Vegetarian society: A group of people who help teach others about a vegetarian diet. A vegetarian society can be a group of people living in the same area who get together to share food and ideas, or it can be a large, national organization with members around the country.

Vitamin B$_{12}$: A vitamin your body needs for proper nervous system functioning.

Vitamin C: A vitamin your body needs for healthy tissues, to heal wounds, and to resist infection. It also helps your body absorb iron from plant foods.

Vivisection: The use of live animals for research experiments.

Whey: A milk-derived ingredient found in many processed foods.

Whole-wheat flour: A light-brown flour made from wheat that still has all its nutritious parts (the bran, germ, and endosperm). Whole-wheat pastry flour is a variety that works well in breads and baked goods.

INDEX

Note: Recipe pages are indicated in **boldface.**

ABOUT THE AUTHOR

A graduate of Northwestern University with a degree from the Medill School of Journalism, Judy Krizmanic is a former editor at *Vegetarian Times* who has written extensively on vegetarian health and nutrition. Currently living in Chicago, Ms. Krizmanic is a freelance writer and a regular contributor to *Vegetarian Times*. *A Teen's Guide to Going Vegetarian* is her first book.